THE ENGLISH GHOST

NON-FICTION

London: The Biography
Albion: The Origins of the English Imagination
The Collection: Journalism, Reviews, Essays, Short Stories, Lectures
edited by Thomas Wright
Thames: Sacred River
Venice: Pure City

FICTION

The Great Fire of London
The Last Testament of Oscar Wilde
Hawksmoor
Chatterton
First Light
English Music
The House of Doctor Dee
Dan Leno and the Limehouse Golem
Milton in America
The Plato Papers
The Clerkenwell Tales
The Lambs of London
The Fall of Troy
The Casebook of Victor Frankenstein

BIOGRAPHY

Ezra Pound and his World
T.S. Eliot
Dickens
Blake
The Life of Thomas More
Shakespeare: The Biography

BRIEF LIVES

Chaucer
J.M.W. Turner
Newton
Poe: A Life Cut Short

The English Ghost

PETER ACKROYD

Chatto & Windus
LONDON

Published by Chatto & Windus 2010

4 6 8 10 9 7 5

Copyright © Peter Ackroyd 2010

First published in Great Britain in 2010 by
Chatto & Windus
Random House, 20 Vauxhall Bridge Road,
London SW1V 2SA
www.rbooks.co.uk

Addresses for companies within The Random House Group Limited can
be found at: www.randomhouse.co.uk/offices.htm

The Random House Group Limited Reg. No. 954009

A CIP catalogue record for this book
is available from the British Library

ISBN 9780701169893

The Random House Group Limited supports The Forest Stewardship
Council (FSC), the leading international forest certification organisation.
All our titles that are printed on Greenpeace approved FSC certified
paper carry the FSC logo. Our paper procurement policy can be found at
www.rbooks.co.uk/environment

Typeset by Palimpsest Book Production Limited,
Falkirk, Stirlingshire
Printed and bound in Great Britain by
Clays Ltd, St Ives plc

Contents

The wandering ghost

Clerical souls

Animal spirits

Moving things

Farewell

The living and the dead

Introduction

ENGLAND IS A HAUNTED COUNTRY. SEVERAL EXPLANATIONS, FOR THE ubiquity of the ghost in this land, can be offered. Alone among the countries of Europe, England is bordered by original British (or Celtic) nations. The popularity of the English ghost tradition – the English see more ghosts than anyone else – is deeply rooted in its peculiar mingling of Germanic, Nordic and British superstitions. The English are also in many respects obsessed with the past, with ruins, with ancient volumes. It is the country where archaeology is placed on national television, and where every town and village has its own local historian. Ghosts therefore may be seen as a bridge of light between the past and the present, or between the living and the dead. They represent continuity, albeit of a spectral kind.

The word is of Anglo-Saxon derivation yet, curiously enough, the Anglo-Saxons did not see ghosts. But they told two strange stories of haunting. One of them occurs in *Beowulf*, where the monstrous figure of Grendel would immediately be understood by medieval listeners as a revenant. Grendel stands apart from life and joy. He is uncanny. He moves through walls, and cannot be touched by sword or spear. His only purpose is to destroy, and the terror he induces is one associated with primal fear of the darkness. The other Anglo-Saxon story is of more solid variety. The famous poem 'The Ruin' opens with the line 'Wraetlic is thaes wealhstane' to be translated as 'Wraith-like is this native stone'. In the stone of England itself lies the wraith. The wraith is an emanation of England. Although the Anglo-Saxons saw no ghosts, they knew themselves to be haunted. The English have a rich repository of words to describe uneasy soil – 'marsh', 'mere', 'mire', 'fen', 'bog' and 'swamp' among them – and it is not at all coincidental that they have also been used to describe the abode of ghostly apparitions.

In the medieval period the English ghosts were deemed to be the souls immured in purgatory, pleading for prayers to absolve them from punishment. They were also happy to proclaim the values of the sacraments, and in particular of confession, extreme unction and infant baptism. Alternatively, ghosts were the spirits of saints sent from God with news of paradise. They could in certain circumstances be the machinations of the devil. In *The Anatomy of Melancholy*, written in the early part of the seventeenth century, Robert Burton argued that 'Divells many times appeare to men, & afright them out of their wits sometimes walking at noone day, sometimes at nights, counterfeiting dead mens ghosts'. In any event, whatever their origin, they were part of the machinery of theology and of the supernatural; they were emanations from the eternal world of bliss and pain beyond the grave. They were an integral part of the communion of the living and the dead that the Church represented.

The doctrines promulgated at the time of the Reformation effectively dispensed with the notions of purgatory and its purging fires. But if there was no such place, then ghosts could hardly claim it as their home. That is why there was a strong tendency, among orthodox churchmen, to dispense with ghosts altogether or to treat them as manifestations of the devil alone. Yet they could not be banished from the earth. The teachings of the Nonconformists tended to credit the existence of ghosts, if only to refute the far more serious phenomenon of atheism. In the middle of the seventeenth century Henry More, in *The Immortality of the Soul*, argued that ghosts were still effective 'in detecting the murderer, in disposing their estates, in rebuking injurious executors, in visiting and counselling their wives and children, in forewarning them of such and such courses, with other matters of like sort'. The late seventeenth and early eighteenth centuries were also the periods in which pamphlets were issued revealing the latest ghostly manifestation; they were generally entitled 'Strange And Extraordinary News From . . .' and their content was attested by numerous witnesses. That stentorian voice of eighteenth-century England, Samuel Johnson, said on the subject of ghosts that 'all argument is against it; but all belief is for it'.

Nineteenth-century England was perhaps the golden age of the ghost. It may have ceased to have any messages or any advice for the living, but it was everywhere. The yearnings associated with the Romantic movement of English poetry found fruition in the spectacle of the melancholy ghost. There was much popular interest in spirit-rappings and in spirit-tappings. The fashion for mesmerism, in the middle of the century, provoked belief in some form of plasma or magnetic fluid that might harbour the forms of spirits. Technological progress also seemed to affirm the existence of spectral bodies, with the appearance of photographs intending to reveal the ghostly occupants of rooms and chairs. The Society for Psychical Research, founded in 1882, lent seriousness and credibility to the quest for spirits. A questionnaire sent out by the society in 1894 revealed that out of seventeen thousand people, 673 claimed that they had seen a ghost in one form or another. It is perhaps curious, however, that the majority of them did not know the identity of the spirit in question. The manifestation appeared arbitrary and purposeless. It is also worth observing that many apparent 'sightings' of ghosts have been discredited, and that many photographs of spirits are the obvious products of fakery. In the field of ghost-hunting there were many frauds and charlatans, intent on producing a sensation rather than a verifiable record.

The twentieth century marks the general popularity of the ghost story in English literature, with the advent of writers such as M. R. James and Algernon Blackwood. The quintessential English ghost story is alarming but also oddly consoling. It is inexplicable and yet perfectly credible. Some comfort, some confirmation of an alternative world, may be derived from the presence of ghosts. The English temperament, in its older manifestations, seemed to waver between the phlegmatic and the melancholy. In the English ghost story itself a matter-of-factness is combined with an intense longing for revelation or for spirituality of the most basic kind. That interest has been maintained in the twenty-first century by the popularity of many television programmes devoted to the subject of haunting and ghost-hunting. It may be said that more people believe in ghosts today than at any other time in England's history.

Other words for ghosts can be found. 'Spook' derives from Iceland, 'dobby' from the Gaelic language and 'wraith' from the Scottish borders. The various names that begin with the prefix 'bug' are of Welsh or Cornish ancestry. Reginald Scot, in *The Discoverie of Witchcraft* published in 1584, remarks upon 'the spook, the man in the oke, the fire-drake, Tom Thombe, Tom Tumbler Boneless and such other BUGS'. The commonplace phrase, 'stop bugging me', can perhaps be translated as 'stop haunting me'. Some ghosts seem to be unique to England, among them the phantom monks and silent nuns who according to G. K. Chesterton come to upbraid the heirs of those who despoiled the monasteries at the time of the Reformation.

There may be intimations of religious guilt in the contemporary sighting of long-dead priests. Also unique to England are the bedroom ghosts, the 'silkies' named after the fact that on passing by they send out a low rustling sound such as that made by silk.

Yet each region of England has its own particular spirits. In Cornwall there was a strong belief in fairies as being part of the community of the dead. Since Cornwall is generally deemed to have been the last haven for 'British' or 'Celtic' people, these beliefs may represent the remnants of a very ancient folk tradition. The Celts do, in general, have more fantastical spirits. In Northumberland they were known as 'dobies' or 'dobbies', a name which derives from the Celtic *dovach* meaning the black, mournful or sorrowful one. Many of these spirits were associated with particular places. There was 'the dobie of Mortham' that walked in a ravine where the River Greta makes its way between Rokeby Park and Mortham. Dobies were known to lurk beneath bridges or ancient towers. Sometimes they would clamber up from beneath the bridges and embrace an unwary traveller. The 'Shotton dobie', by the River Dee, took the form of a large bird like a goose that would accompany travellers on the road before flying off with loud screams. The inhabitants of the neighbourhood refused to frighten it or disturb it for, in the words reported, *'they knew what it was'*.

Some dobies were more benevolent; they were known to be attached to particular houses or farms, where they would labour on behalf of the families that dwelled there. They were characteristically given similar nicknames, such as 'Old Flam' or 'Old Clegg'. 'Old' suggests that these were spirits of long duration in the same place.

In south-western England ghosts were known as 'hobs'. They often performed the role of nightwatchmen, and under cover of night and darkness their footsteps could be heard. One Somersetshire woman became so accustomed to the tread that she would call out

'Hello there, I'm quite all right, thank you.' Then the hob would depart. The Holman Clavel Inn in Taunton had its own hob known as 'Old Charlie'. The owners were alerted to his presence when they heard from time to time the noise of skittles in the next-door room; when they went to investigate, no one was playing. Glasses, left on the counter of the bar overnight to dry, were returned to their proper places. Clean linen was pressed and folded.

In Yorkshire and in the North Midlands spirits were also known as 'hobs' or 'hobbits'. They were popularly supposed to haunt caves, bridges and round barrows; but they were, in particular, associated with specific places. Thus there was Lealholm Hob and Scugdale Hob. There was a Hob Lane and a Hob Bridge at Gatley in Lancashire. Several Hob Lanes can still be found in Warwickshire.

In the north of England the ghosts were often known as 'boggarts'. This is derived from *bwg*, the Celtic word for ghost, and can be heard in better-known words such as 'bugbear' and 'bogeyman'. It is also behind the Cornish hobgoblin Bucca and Shakespeare's Puck. They had a habit of pinching or biting those whom they haunted, and were renowned for their custom of crawling into the beds of their victims. Sometimes they shook the hangings of the beds, or rustled among discarded clothes. More seriously, they would snatch up sleeping infants and deposit them on the stones outside. There was a boggart often seen and heard in Thackergate, near Alderdale, now gone, that frightened some people out of their wits. Boggarts haunted places where there had been a violent death.

It was said that, if you could see a boggart, it would become visible to your companions if you touched them. The only way of removing these apparitions was by means of fire; flame destroyed them, or frightened them away. So we have reports of their last words — 'It was time for us to come out!' or 'We have flitted! We have gone away!' They lived also in caves and valleys. They were believed to perch in yew trees. An area of open ground within Manchester, once a deep dell covered with trees, is still known as Boggart Hole Clough. Another Boggart Hole exists in Oldham.

The spirits who inhabited old forts, castles and dungeons were known as 'powries' or 'dunters'. They made a noise as of beating flax, or bruising barley in the hollow of a stone. In Durham there was a creature called 'the brag'. One old lady told William Brockie, author of *The Legends and Superstitions of Durham* (1886), that 'I never saw the brag very distinctly, but I frequently heard it. It sometimes appeared like a calf with a white handkerchief about its neck and a bushy tail; it came also like a galloway [a breed of horse], but more often like a coach horse . . . My brother once saw it like four men holding up a white sheet.' The precision of her observations is in marked contrast to the strangeness of that made by her brother. In the same period it was reported that the midwives of the district were always accompanied on their ministrations by a galloway.

There are other names for apparitions, including 'shellycoats' and 'scrags', 'fetches' and 'mum-pokers', 'spoorns' and 'melch-dicks', 'larrs', 'ouphs' and 'old-shocks'. There are 'swathes' and 'scar-bugs', 'bolls' and 'gringes', 'nickies' and 'freits', 'chittifaces' and 'clabbernappers'. In fact there are more than two hundred ways of describing the ghosts of England, a testament if nothing else to their ubiquity and their variety. There is also another expression. When a young woman in Shropshire screamed out 'There's the *know* of a dog', she meant that she had seen the shape of a dog when no living dog was there. The '*know*' of anything is its spectral appearance. Another word for a ghost is 'token'. In Shropshire a phantom was called a 'frittenin'' as in the remark that 'since then there has always been frittenin' under this tree'. Another expression from the same region, 'There's summat to be seen', is meant to convey the presence of the unnatural.

*

Flames turn blue; dogs howl; a sound of rustling silk can be heard; the temperature is lowered. These are some of the signs of a haunting. Ghosts are not welcomed. The people to whom a ghost has appeared often recall that they could not speak at the moment of seeing. 'I dare not speak,' one witness wrote. 'I was afraid of the sound of my own voice.'

'Balls' of light have been observed at the time of alleged sightings or disturbances. A case from 1870 states that 'a large luminous ball floated, increasing in size, from under her bed'. A modern investigator, speaking in 2007, described 'a very visible luminescent ball' appearing. From an account of a haunting in 1850 we read that 'luminous balls seemed to go up and towards a trap-door in the ceiling which led to the roof of the cottage'.

A report, from a hotel that in 1966 was besieged by unusual phenomena, records one occasion when a 'ball of fluorescent mist' drifted past a group of spectators before vanishing through a doorway into the street. In another modern setting, where a married couple had been separately disturbed by an apparition and by the sound of scratching, the husband reported seeing a ball of light changing size constantly and floating around the living room. Catherine Crowe, in *The Night Side of Nature* (1848), wrote that 'I meet with innumerable cases in which this phosphorescent light is one of the accompaniments' of unusual activity. She reported one case where a ball of flickering light caused 'excessive trembling' in the person who witnessed it; this was followed by 'the complete doubling up of his whole body into a round ball'. It has been suggested that these hovering or floating lights, well attested in many accounts, are some wayward form of energy. It has even been surmised that they are somehow produced and controlled by human agency, but no plausible explanation has ever been offered for their shape or nature.

The curious phenomenon of the 'will o' the wisp' or 'corpse

candle' is still intriguing. It has often been suggested that it represents nothing more than the gaseous emanation from some rotting matter; this is a seductive, and even plausible, theory but it is no more than a theory. The connection has never been proved. It is a hypothesis, not a conclusion. Then there is the testimony of the nineteenth-century poet John Clare, who had known of 'bog vapours' throughout his childhood in Northamptonshire. But then he saw two of them seeming to play one with other and the sight 'robd me of the little philosophical reasoning which I had about them. I now believe them spirits.'

Noises are often the first inklings of a haunting. Knockings and tappings are frequent. The sound of footsteps is common. There are many reports of unseen visitors scraping the floor, as if they were covered with branches, or apparently dragging someone or something. The jingling of money is common. A person seems to be dragging furniture about the rooms, although the house is empty. Calls and cries have been heard. There may be the sound of laughter, of a newspaper rustling, of a dog growling. On the wall of a medieval manor house in Hertfordshire, Hinxworth Place, there was once a sign inscribed upon a wall – 'This is where a monk was buried alive in this wall. His cries can be heard sometimes at midnight. 1770.'

In Richard Bovet's *Pandaemonium*, published in the late seventeenth century, we read that 'a little after I was got into Bed, I heard something walk about the Room, like a Woman with a Tabby Gown trailing about the Room; it made a mighty rushelling noise, but I could see nothing'. The narrator also records that a little later 'it seemed to groan, and draw a great Chair with its foot'. In a farmhouse overlooking the Lamorna Valley in west Cornwall, there was a chamber from which issued the sound of an old spinning wheel. It is only one of a number of cases in which the sounds of ancient occupations can clearly be heard still echoing. Cornish tin miners, from the seventeenth century forward, have been sure that they heard the noises of small hammers in parts of the mine where there was no activity. The phantoms were known as 'knockers' or 'buccas'. When the sounds were heard, there was to be no more whistling or swearing; nothing was to be marked with a cross.

Then there are the voices. Andrew Lang tells us the story of a young lady who was in her bath when she heard a voice saying 'Open the door' four times. She did so, and thereupon fainted. There was no one there. A woman rose up among cattle, in a farmyard, and said, 'Never mind it John, you do your work and I will do mine.' The head of a martyred medieval saint called out 'Here, here, here' to those who sought it.

But many spectres cannot speak. It is commonly reported that ghosts are on the point of saying something, but unaccountably cannot. Some among them seem to be physically prevented from talking. Characteristically they gasp or emit a low and garbled sound.

Many stories in this volume concern the activity of the lively spirits generally known as poltergeists. They are similar, one to another, in ways that suggest a genuine and distinctive phenomenon. Their presence is reported in the twelfth century, in the chronicles of Gerald of Wales, when certain spirits threw objects and cut holes in the clothes of unsuspecting victims. Precisely the same activities are described in modern poltergeists. One other curious resemblance can be found between the various accounts. It is often remarked that the flying objects, when they hit human beings, do no hurt or injure. They land softly. Yet when they hit walls or doors, they do visible damage.

Do ghosts smell? Some have claimed that they smell of stale food. Or, perhaps, of rotting food. Others claim to have a detected a 'fetid' smell in the presence of apparitions. Yet that may be fanciful, a reminder of the association of ghosts with death. Rooms are suddenly filled with the smell of fresh cigar smoke. Floating perfumes issue from no visible source. And there are fugitive smells, of leather-working or brewing, that seem to hover in premises that were once devoted to a particular trade. Certain churches and abbeys are filled with an inexplicable odour of incense; this has been particularly remarked among the ruins of Glastonbury. In old buildings there may be the sudden emanation of the odour of herbs. The scent of thyme is supposed to be an indication of murder. There are cases involving the sudden and overwhelming fragrance of flowers.

Ghosts are sometimes seen at the moment of the death of the person. There are also ghosts of the living, often seen many miles from the location of the human being. Ghosts of the living also appear when the living subject is asleep or dreaming. Some ghosts appear as animals. The black dog or 'shuck' was well known before Johnson borrowed it as an image of melancholy. Other ghosts come back because they have not been properly buried. There are ghosts who return to correct a wrong, or to fulfil a pledge. Some seem sent merely to cause mischief and alarm. But the vast majority of ghosts seem to be without a purpose. More than one witness has described them as 'mindless' or 'brainless'. The ghost is normally seen by one person rather than a group of people. They can touch you, but you cannot touch them.

Our ancestors did not use the word 'exorcise' to describe the containment or banishment of ghosts; they spoke of 'laying' them, as if they are requested to sleep rather than being driven away. The laying of ghosts, in previous centuries, followed a customary pattern. The minister, when called to eliminate a spirit, was asked to 'read it down'. By the light of candles the priest would read from the Bible, in the process diminishing the ghost in size until it could be placed in a bottle or box. The other form of laying a ghost was by incessant prayer, sometimes lasting for several days and nights. There is an account of one ghost 'who refused to go into the bottle in which it was to be imprisoned, because there was a man outside eating bread and cheese . . . the poor minister was so exhausted by the task that he died'. The bottle containing the ghost might then thrown into a pond or pool; alternatively the ghost might be consigned to a tree or to a chimney. The usual duration of this exile was sixty-six or ninety-nine years. Yet a ghost under Eardisland Bridge in Herefordshire has been laid for the last two thousand years.

The other method of laying a ghost was to command it to perform an impossible task, such as weaving ropes of sand or emptying a pond with a sieve. Some ghosts, however, cannot be laid to rest. Wherever they are taken they are allowed to move back to the site of their haunting at the pace of one 'cock-stride' each year.

It was believed in some regions that the best method of exorcising a ghost was to throw graveyard earth at it. Earth from a graveyard was believed to be potent because it could dissolve human flesh. It is said that ghosts also have an aversion to iron. This superstition is suggestive. It would seem to have arisen in the neolithic period when the mineral may have been an object of wonder and fear, its properties held to be magical. If this is indeed the case, then the belief in ghosts or spirits extends a long way back. The manner of address to a ghost, in previous centuries, was also laid down by custom. 'In the name of God, what art thou?' A priest might say, 'In the name of God, why do you trouble us?'

'There is no people, rude or learned,' Imlac declares in Samuel Johnson's *Rasselas*, 'among whom apparitions of the dead are not related and believed. Those that never heard of one another would not have agreed in a tale which nothing but experience can make credible.' On just such a principle the stories in this volume have been collected. It is merely stating the obvious to observe that the witnesses here fully believed in the reality of what they had seen or experienced. Whether the reader chooses to believe in it is another matter.

The phantom in the house

The events in Hinton Manor

In January 1765 Mr and Mrs Ricketts assumed the tenancy of Hinton Manor, in Hampshire; the owner and previous occupant had been Henry Bilson-Legge, who on his death in 1764 had been hailed on his tombstone as 'enlivened with a peculiar vein of the most striking wit'. His daughter, who on her marriage had become Lady Stawell, did not care to reside in the house and was delighted to procure tenants for it.

The Ricketts were at first happy in their residence, but they soon became alarmed by the frequent opening and shutting of doors during the night. Mrs Ricketts feared that there were 'irregularities' on the part of the servants, but having made the strictest enquiries she was disabused of that notion. Then her husband, fearing that a stranger had obtained the keys of the house, arranged that all the locks should be changed. But the noise of closing, or slamming, doors continued as before. There were other unusual events. Two visitors to the house, on separate occasions, declared that they had seen a figure in a 'snuff-coloured' coat; the figure had been glimpsed both inside and outside the house. In addition, the servants, assembled in the kitchen for a meal, observed a woman in a dark dress of silk rushing past them and going out into the yard. A handyman, coming through the door at the same time, had seen nothing.

Then the manifestations ceased. For two or three years there were no more abnormal or inexplicable events at Hinton Manor, and in 1769 Mr Ricketts sailed to Jamaica in order to administer the land and property he owned there. He left behind his wife and three children, together with a retinue of eight servants. Soon after his departure, however, the noises began again. Mrs Ricketts was so convinced of the reality of these sounds that she began to keep a record of their occurrence. In the summer of 1770, when 'lying in the yellow bedchamber, I plainly heard the footsteps of a man, with plodding step, walking towards the foot of my bed'. She sprang out of bed, thoroughly alarmed by the sound, and took refuge in the adjoining nursery; she returned to her room with the nurse, and a light, but nothing could be seen. The sound of plodding footsteps was subsequently heard in her room on more than one occasion; her maid's room was similarly affected. Another abnormal sound also seemed to emanate from within the house, described by Mrs Ricketts as 'a hollow murmuring that seemed to possess the whole house; it was independent of wind, being equally heard on the calmest night'.

On a subsequent night Mrs Ricketts heard the front door being slammed with such force that the walls of her bedroom – above the hall – shook perceptibly. On investigation, the front door was locked and bolted as usual. The unusual episodes increased in strength and frequency throughout that summer. The sounds 'began before I went to bed, and with intermissions were heard till after broad day in the morning'. The noise now included that of human voices. 'A shrill female voice would begin,' Mrs Ricketts wrote, 'and then two others with deeper and manlike tones seemed to join in the discourse.' She was lying in bed one night, when 'I heard the most loud, deep, tremendous noise, which seemed to rush and fall with infinite velocity on the lobby floor'. This was followed by 'a shrill and dreadful shriek . . . repeated three or four times'.

Mrs Ricketts now felt that the situation had become dangerous to the health of the whole family and its servants. Her husband was still detained in Jamaica but by great good fortune her brother, Admiral Jervis, had just sailed into Portsmouth and had determined to visit Hinton Manor. On being told the story, he harboured doubts about any supernatural agency. With a friend, Mr Luttrell, he decided to stay up for several nights with a pistol. They stationed themselves in different rooms, and waited.

The noises, of shrieks and of footsteps, began as before. Both men rushed out of their rooms, pistols at the ready, but there was nothing visible. Convinced now of the truth of his sister's story, Admiral Jervis advised her to leave the house as soon as possible. She never returned.

A small note was added to the transcript of this story. A later resident of Hinton Manor wrote that 'my mother-in-law [Lady Sherborne] remembers when about 6 years old [*circa* 1786] while staying at Hinton being awoke in the night and carried down to the Rectory as the noises were so great Lady Stawell could not remain in the house'.

The glass tube

This is the memoir of Edward Lenthal Swifte, Keeper of the Crown Jewels in the first half of the nineteenth century.

'In 1814 I was appointed Keeper of the Crown Jewels in the Tower, where I resided with my family until my retirement in 1852. One Saturday night in October 1817, I was at supper with my wife, her sister, and our little boy, in the sitting room of the Jewel House. The room was — as it still is — irregularly shaped, having three doors and two windows, which last are cut nearly nine feet deep into the outer wall; between these there is a chimney-piece projecting far into the room, and (then) surmounted with a large oil-picture. On the night in question, the doors were all closed, heavy and dark cloth curtains were let down over the windows, and the only light in the room was that of two candles on the table. I sat at the foot of the table, my son on my right hand, his mother fronting the chimney-piece, and her sister on the opposite side. I had offered a glass of wine and water to my wife when, on putting it to her lips, she paused and exclaimed, "Good God! What is that?" I looked up and saw a cylindrical figure, like a glass tube, seemingly about the thickness of my arm, and hovering between the ceiling and the table; its contents appeared to be a dense fluid, white and pale azure, like the gathering of a summer cloud, and incessantly mingling within the cylinder. This lasted about two minutes, when it slowly began to move before my sister-in-law; then, following the oblong shape of the table, *before* my son and myself; passing *behind* my wife, it paused for a moment over her right shoulder (observe, there was no mirror opposite to her in which she could there behold it). Instantly she crouched down, and with both hands covering her shoulder, she shrieked out, "Oh Christ! It has seized me!" Even now, while writing, I feel the fresh horror of that moment. I caught up my chair, struck at the wainscot behind her, rushed upstairs to the children's room, and told the terrified nurse what I had seen. Meanwhile the other domestics had hurried into the parlour, where their mistress recounted to them the scene, even as I was detailing it upstairs.'

There is a postscript to this story, again recounted by Mr Swifte. It took place a few days after the apparition of the glass tube.

'One of the night sentries at the Jewel House, a man who was in perfect health and spirits, and was singing and whistling up to the moment of the occurrence, was alarmed by a figure like a huge bear issuing from under the Jewel Room door. He thrust at it with his bayonet, which stuck in the door, even as my chair had dinted the wainscot; he dropped in a fit, and was carried senseless to the guardroom.

'When on the morrow I saw the unfortunate soldier in the main guardroom, his fellow sentinel was also there, and testified to having seen him at his post just before the alarm, awake and alert, and had even spoken to him. I saw the unfortunate man again on the following day, but changed beyond my recognition; in another day or two, the brave and steady soldier, who would have mounted a breach or led a forlorn hope with unshaken nerves, *died* — at the presence of a shadow.'

The Cheltenham ghost

IN THE SPRING OF 1882 CAPTAIN DESPARD AND HIS FAMILY RENTED A house in Cheltenham; it was of moderate size, built in the fashion of the 1860s on the site of a market garden. There was nothing out of the ordinary about it, and it was essentially commonplace, but it was not lucky with its occupants. It had previously been inhabited by Mr S——, an Anglo-Indian, who on the death of his young wife in the house took to the bottle. He married again, but his new wife could not break his addiction to drink; indeed she also succumbed to it. There were violent arguments between them, particularly over the care and education of the four young children of Mr S——'s first marriage. Mr S—— also hid his previous wife's jewellery under the floorboards of the small front sitting room, as a form of dowry to his children. His second wife left the house after a particularly violent quarrel and removed herself to Clifton. A few months later, on 14 July 1876, Mr S—— died in the house. It was purchased soon after by an elderly gentleman, Mr L——, who died six months after moving into the house; curiously enough he died in the same small sitting room where Mr S—— had died and where Mr S—— had concealed his first wife's jewels.

This is the history of the house before the arrival of Captain

Despard and his family five years later. The house had been difficult to rent out in the interim. His daughter, Miss R. C. Despard, nineteen at the time of the events here related, can take up the story.

'We moved in towards the end of April, and it was not until the following June that I first saw the apparition. I had gone up to my room, but was not yet in bed, when I heard someone at the door, and went to it, thinking that it might be my mother. On opening the door, I saw no one; but on going a few steps along the passage, I saw the figure of a tall lady, dressed in black, standing at the head of the stairs. After a few moments she descended the stairs, and I followed for a short distance, feeling curious about what it could be. I had only a small piece of candle, and it suddenly burnt itself out; and, being unable to see more, I went back to my room.

'The figure was that of a tall lady, dressed in black of a soft woollen material, judging from the slight sound in moving. The face was hidden by a handkerchief held in the right hand. This is all I noticed then; but on further occasions, when I was able to observe her more closely, I saw the upper part of the left side of the forehead, and a little of the hair above. Her left hand was nearly hidden by her sleeve and a fold of her dress. As she held it down a portion of a widow's cuff was visible on both wrists, so that the whole impression was that of a lady in widow's weeds. There was no cap on the head but a general effect of blackness suggests a bonnet, with a long veil or hood.

'During the next two years – from 1882 to 1884 – I saw the figure; at first at long intervals, and afterwards at shorter, but I only mentioned these appearances to one friend, who did not speak of them to anyone.

'During this period, as far as we know, there were only three appearances to anyone else. The first, in the summer of 1882, was to my sister, Mrs K—, when the figure was thought to be that of a Sister of Mercy who had called at the house, and no further curiosity was aroused. My sister was coming down the stairs rather late for dinner at 6.30, it then being quite light, when she saw the figure cross the hall in front of her and pass into the drawing room. She then asked the rest of us, already seated at dinner, "Who was that Sister of Mercy whom I have just seen going into the drawing room?" She was told that there was no such person, and a servant was sent to look; but the drawing room was empty, and she was sure no one had come in. Mrs K— persisted that she had seen a tall figure in black, with some white about it; but nothing further was thought of the matter.

'The second appearance, in the autumn of 1883, was seen by the housemaid about 10 p.m., she declaring that someone had got into the house, her description agreeing fairly with what I had seen; but as on searching no one was found, her story received no credit.

'On or about December 18, 1883, it was seen in the drawing room by my brother and another little boy. They were playing outside the terrace when they saw the figure in the drawing room close to the window, and ran in to see who it could be that was crying so bitterly. They found no one in the drawing room, and the parlour-maid told them that no one had come into the house.

'After the first time, I followed the figure several times downstairs into the drawing room, where she remained a variable time, generally standing to the right-hand side of the bow window. From the drawing room she went along the passage towards the garden door, where she always disappeared.

'The first time I spoke to her was on 29 January 1884. I opened the drawing-room door softly and went in, standing just by it. She came in past me and walked to the sofa and stood still there, so I went up to her and asked if I could help her. She moved, and I thought she was going to speak, but she only gave a slight gasp and moved towards the door. Just by the door I spoke to her again, but she seemed as if she were quite unable to speak. She walked into the hall, then by the side door she seemed to disappear as before. In May and June, 1884, I tried some experiments, fastening string with marine glue across the stairs at different heights from the ground.

'I also attempted to touch her, but she always eluded me. It was not that there was nothing there to touch, but that she always seemed to be *beyond* me, and, if followed into a corner, simply disappeared.

'During these two years the only *noises* I heard were those of slight pushes against my bedroom door, accompanied by footsteps; and if I looked out on hearing these sounds, I invariably saw the figure. Her footstep was very light, you could hardly hear it, except on the linoleum, and then only like a person walking softly with thin boots on. The appearances during the next two months, July and August 1884, became much more frequent; indeed they were then at their maximum from which time they seem gradually to have decreased, until now they seem to have ceased.

'On July 21 I went into the drawing room where my father and sisters were sitting, about nine in the evening, and sat down on a couch close to the bow window. A few minutes later, as I sat reading, I saw the figure come in at the open door, cross the room and take up a position close behind the couch where I was. I was astonished that no one else in the room saw her, as she was so very distinct to me. My youngest brother, who had before seen her, was not in the room. She stood behind the couch for about half an hour, and then as usual walked to the door. I went after her, on the excuse of getting a book, and saw her pass along the hall, until she came to the garden door, where she disappeared. I spoke to her as she passed the foot of the stairs, but she did not answer, although as before she stopped and seemed as though *about* to speak. On July 31 some time after I had gone up to bed, my second sister E., who had remained downstairs talking in another sister's room, came to me saying that someone had passed her on the stairs. I tried then to persuade her that it was one of the servants, but next morning found that it could not have been so, as none of them had been out of their rooms at that hour, and E.'s more detailed description tallied with what I had seen.

'On the night of August 1 I again saw the figure. I heard the footsteps outside on the landing about 2 a.m. I got up at once, and went outside. She was then at the end of the landing at the top of the stairs, then went downstairs, stopping again when she reached the hall below. I opened the drawing-room door and she went in, walked across the room to the couch in the bow window, stayed there a little while, then came out of the room, went along the passage, and disappeared by the garden door. I spoke to her again, but she did not answer.

'On the night of August 2 the footsteps were heard by my three sisters and by the cook, all of whom slept on the top landings – also by my married sister, Mrs K., who was sleeping on the floor below. They all said the next morning that they had heard them very plainly pass and repass their doors.

'The cook was a middle-aged and very sensible person; she told me that she had heard these footsteps before, and that she had seen the figure on the stairs one night when going down to the kitchen to fetch hot water after the servants had come up to bed. She described it as a lady in a widow's dress, tall and slight, with her face hidden in a handkerchief held in her right hand. Unfortunately we have since lost sight of this servant; she left us about a year afterwards on her mother's death, and we cannot now trace her. She also saw the figure outside the kitchen windows on the terrace walk, she herself being in the kitchen.

'These footsteps are very characteristic; and not at all like those of any of the people in the house; they are soft and rather slow, though decided and even. My sisters would not go out on the landing after hearing them pass, nor would the servants, but each time when I have gone out after hearing them, I have seen the figure there.

'On August 5 I told my father about her and what we had seen and heard. He was much astonished, not having seen or heard anything himself at that time – neither then had my mother, but she is slightly deaf, and is an invalid.

'On August 6 a neighbour, General A., who lived opposite, sent his son to enquire after my married sister, as he had seen a lady crying in our orchard, which is visible from the road. He had described her to his son, and afterwards to us, as a tall lady in black, and a bonnet with a long veil, crying, with a handkerchief held up to her face. He did not know my sister by sight, as she had only been with us a few days, but he knew that she was in mourning for her baby son. My sister was not in the orchard that day, is rather short, and wore no veil.

'The same evening this General A. came over to our house, and we all took up various stations on the watch for the figure, which, however, was not seen by anyone.

'That night my brother-in-law and sister distinctly heard footsteps first going up the stairs and then down. This was about 2 a.m.

'On the evening of August 12, while coming up the garden, I walked towards the orchard, when I saw the figure cross the orchard, go along the carriage drive in front of the house, and in at the open side door, across the hall, and into the drawing room, I following. She crossed the drawing room and took up her usual position behind the couch in the bow window. My father came in soon after, and I told him she was there. He could not see the figure, but went up to where I showed him she was. She then went swiftly round behind him, across the room, out of the door, and along the hall, disappearing as usual near the garden door, we both following her. We looked out into the garden, having first to unlock the garden door, which my father had locked as he came through, but we saw nothing of her.

'On the same evening, about 8 p.m., and still quite light, my sister E. was singing in the back drawing room. I heard her stop abruptly, come out into the hall and call me. She said she had seen the figure in the drawing room, close behind her as she sat at the piano. I went back into the room with her, and saw the figure in the bow window in her usual place. I spoke to her several times, but had no answer. She stood there for about ten minutes or a quarter of an hour; then went across the room to the door, and along the passage, disappearing in the same place by the same door. My sister M. then came in from the garden, saying she had seen her coming up the kitchen steps outside. We all three then went out in to the garden, when Mrs K. called out from a window on the first storey that she had just seen her pass across the lawn in front, and along the carriage drive towards the orchard. This evening, then, altogether four people saw her. My father was then away, and my youngest brother was out . . .'

In the following year the sound of footsteps was accompanied on occasions by 'heavy thuds and bumpings'. Miss Despard goes on to note that 'the bumps against the bedroom door were so marked as to terrify a new servant, who had heard nothing of the haunting, into the belief that burglars were breaking into her room, while another servant, who had a slight attack of facial hemiplegia, attributed it to attempts at her door worse than usual one night; the doctor, however, thought the attack was caused by cold rather than by fright'. Captain Despard swore the whole family to secrecy, however, in case the landlord suffered from depreciation in the value of the property.

At night, on a later occasion, two of the Despard girls, 'L.' and 'M.', 'opened their door to say that they had heard noises, and also seen what they described as the flame of a candle, without candle or hand visible, cross the room diagonally from corner to door. Two of the maids opened the doors of their two bedrooms, and said that they had also heard noises; they all stood at their doors with their lighted candles for some little time. They all heard steps walking up and down the landing between them; as they passed they felt a sensation which they described as "a cold wind", though their candles were not blown about. They *saw* nothing.'

From 1887 to 1889 the figure was very seldom seen, and the noises abated. From 1889 onwards the phenomena in the house stopped altogether. In her later reflections Miss Despard commented upon 'the impossibility of touching the figure. I have repeatedly followed it into a corner, when it disappeared, and have tried suddenly to pounce upon it, but have never succeeded in touching or getting my hand up to it, the figure eluding my touch.' She also noted that 'although no one had ever seen the second Mrs S— several people who had known her identified her from our description'. The second Mrs S— was the wife who had departed for Clifton a few months before the death of her husband. Miss Despard recollected that 'on being shown a photo album containing a number of portraits, I picked out one of her sister as being more like that of the figure, and was afterwards told that the sisters were much alike'. She noted that the dogs of the household, not the cats, were affected by the phenomena. Of her Skye terrier she described how 'it jumped up, fawning as it would do if a person had been standing there, but suddenly slunk away with its tail between its legs, and retreated, trembling, under a sofa'.

This is the substance of Miss Despard's detailed and careful account; it was compiled from diaries and from letters to her close friend, Catherine Campbell, that she wrote at the time. The several witnesses were subsequently interviewed by Mr Myers of the Society for

Psychical Research. Myers himself noted that 'the phenomena as seen and heard by all the witnesses were very uniform in character'. There are statements from the other members of the Despard family, and from the servants of the house. At the end of her account, Miss Despard also described her feelings on glimpsing the apparition. At first it induced in her 'the feeling of awe at something unknown'; then, after becoming more familiar with the phenomenon, 'I felt conscious of a feeling of *loss,* as if I had lost power to the figure.'

The whiskered gentleman

The following report appeared in the *Bristol Times* from some date in 1846.

'We have this week a ghost story to relate. Yes, a real ghost story without, as yet, any clue as to its elucidation. After the dissolution of an old couple known as the Calendars their ancient residence, adjoining and almost forming a part of All Saints' Church, Bristol, was converted into a vicarage house, and it is still called by that name, though the incumbents have for many years ceased to reside there.

'The present occupants are Mr and Mrs Jones, the sexton and sextoness of the church, and one or two lodgers; and it is to the former and their servant-maid that the strange visitor has made his appearance, causing such terror by his nightly calls, that all three of them have determined upon quitting the premises, if indeed they have not already carried their resolution into effect. Mr and Mrs Jones's description of the disturbance as given to the landlord, on whom they called in great consternation, is as distinct as any ghost story could be.

'The nocturnal visitor is heard walking about the house when the inhabitants are in bed; and Mr Jones, who is by no means of a nervous constitution, declares he has several times seen a light flickering on one of the walls. Mrs Jones is equally certain that she has heard a man with creaking shoes walking in the bedroom above her own, when no man was on the premises (or at least ought not to be) and "was nearly killed with the fright".

'To the maid-servant, however, was vouchsafed the unenvied honour of seeing this restless night visitor; she declares she has repeatedly had her bedroom door unbolted at night, between the hours of twelve and two o'clock, by something in human semblance. She cannot particularise his dress, but describes it as something antique. She further says that he is "a whiskered gentleman" (we give her own words), which whiskered gentleman has gone to the length of shaking her bed, and, she believes, would have shaken herself also, but that she invariably puts her head under the clothes when she sees him approach. Mrs Jones declares she believes in the appearance of the whiskered gentleman, and she had made up her mind the night before she called on her landlord to leap out of the window (and it is not a trifle that will make people leap out of windows) as soon as he entered the room. The effect of the "flickering light" on Mr Jones was quite terrific, causing excessive trembling, and the complete doubling up of his whole body into a round ball.'

The old staircase

The following letters, dated 17 September 1909, were sent to Viscount Halifax by Sir George Sitwell and Lady Ida Sitwell. The events they relate took place in Renishaw, then the home of the Sitwells in Derbyshire, erected in 1625. The first comes from the pen of Sir George.

'Last Saturday two ghosts were seen at Renishaw. Lady Ida had been to Scarborough to attend the Life Boat Ball, at which she had sat up until four o'clock in the morning, returning home in the afternoon. After dinner the party of six – I was absent for a few hours – sat in the drawing room upstairs, Lady Ida lying on a sofa facing the open door.

'She had been speaking to a friend who was sitting on her left when she looked up and saw in the passage outside the figure of a woman, apparently a servant, with grey hair and a white cap, the upper part of her dress being blue and the skirt dark. Her arms were stretched out at full length and the hands were clasped. This figure moved with a very slow, furtive, gliding motion, as if wishing to escape notice, straight towards the head of the old staircase, which I removed twenty years ago. On reaching it, she disappeared.

'Unwilling to think that there was anything supernatural in the appearance, Lady Ida called out "Who's that?" and then the name of the housekeeper. When no one answered she cried to those who were nearest the door, "Run out and see who it is. Run out at once."

'Two people rushed out, but no one was to be seen, nor when the others joined them and searched the hall and passages upstairs could they find anyone resembling the woman described to them by Lady Ida.

'They had given up the search, and were returning to the drawing room, when one of the party, Miss R., who was a little behind the others, exclaimed, "I do believe that's the ghost!" No one else saw anything, but afterwards she described what she had seen. In the full light of the archway below, within twenty feet of her, and just where the door of the old ghost room used to stand, until I removed it and put the present staircase in its place, she saw the figure of a lady, with dark hair and dress, apparently lost in painful thought and oblivious to everything about her. Her dress was fuller than is the modern fashion and the figure, although opaque, cast no shadow. It moved with a curious gliding motion into the darkness and melted away at the spot within a yard of the place where a doorway, now walled up, led from a staircase to the hall. There is no doubt that these figures were actually seen as described.'

Sir George Sitwell goes on to speculate that the figures were 'phantasms' rather than ghosts and that they were 'reversed impressions of something seen in the past'. Lady Ida Sitwell also wrote to Viscount Halifax.

'I saw the figure with such distinctness that I had no doubt at all I was looking at a real person, while, at the same time, although seated in a well-lighted room and chatting with friends, I was conscious of an uneasy, creepy feeling. I tried to see the features, but could not. Even before I called out, my friends noticed that I appeared to be following something with my eyes. The light in the passage was good and I could see so well that I could distinguish the exact shade of the dress. The figures was that of a woman between fifty and sixty years of age and her grey hair was done up in a "bun" under an old-fashioned cap. I had never seen a ghost, nor had I been thinking about ghosts.'

There is a postscript to this story. Twenty-four years before, Sir George Sitwell held a party in celebration of his coming of age. One of the guests was Miss Tait, the daughter of the Archbishop of Canterbury. She had been accommodated in the room at the head of the staircase, later removed, and in the middle of the night she rushed into the room of Sir George's sister claiming that she had been rudely woken by the sensation of 'someone giving her three cold kisses'. She asked Miss Sitwell to come back to the room with her. Miss Sitwell refused on the grounds that, sleeping in the same room, she had once experienced exactly the same sensation. Sir George mentioned this coincidence to his agent, Mr Turnbull, in a light-hearted manner. 'Well, Sir George,' Mr Turnbull replied, 'you may make a joke about it, but when you lent us the house for our honeymoon, Miss Crane, a schoolfellow of my wife's, came to stay with us, and she had the same room and exactly the same experience.' It was for this reason, perhaps, that the room was subsequently removed.

The corpse in Spitalfields

ABOUT THE YEAR 1611 THERE LIVED IN SPITALFIELDS ONE MRS ANNE
Stephenson, a person at that time well known and respected for her
great dealings with the mercers on Ludgate-hill. This person sitting
one evening in her house alone, and musing upon business, happened
by accident to look behind her when, to her great surprise, she saw,
as it were, a dead corpse, as she thought, lying extended upon the
floor, just as a dead body should be, excepting that the foot of one
leg was fixed on the ground as it is in bed, when one lies with one
knee up; she looked at it awhile, and by degrees withdrew her eyes
from so unpleasing an object: however a strange kind of air of curiosity
soon overcame her fears, and she ventured a second time to look
that way, and saw it a considerable time longer fixed as before; but
she durst not stir from her seat. She again turned from the horrible
and melancholy spectacle, and, resuming her courage, after a little
reflection, got up with a design to ascertain herself of the reality of
the vision by going nearer to it; but it was vanished!

Dr Johnson's friend

TALKING OF GHOSTS, DR JOHNSON SAID HE KNEW ONE FRIEND, WHO WAS an honest man, who told him he had seen a ghost; old Mr Edward Cave, the printer, at St John's Gate. He said Mr Cave did not like to talk of it, and seemed to be in great horror whenever it was mentioned. Boswell said, 'Pray, sir, what did he say was the appearance?' Johnson replied, 'Why, sir, something of a shadowy being.'

BOSWELL: 'Was there not a story of the ghost of Parson Ford having appeared?'

JOHNSON: 'Sir, it was believed. A waiter at Hummums, in which Ford died, had been absent for some time and returned, not knowing Ford was dead: going down to the cellar, according to the story, he met him; going down again, he met him a second time. When he came up and asked some of the people of the house what Ford could be doing there? They told him Ford was dead. The waiter took a fever, in which he lay some time: when he recovered he said he had a message to deliver to some women from Ford, but he was not to tell what or to whom. He walked out; he was followed, but somewhere about St Paul's they lost him; he came back and said he had delivered the message, and the women exclaimed, "Then we are all undone!" Dr Pellet, who was not a credulous man, inquired into the truth of this story, and said the evidence was irresistible. My wife went to Hummums (it is a place where people get themselves cupped); I believe she went with the intention to hear about this story of Ford. At first they were unwilling to tell her; but, after they had talked to her, she came away satisfied that it was true. To be sure the man had a fever, and this vision may have been the beginning of it; but, if the message to the women and their behaviour upon it were true, as related, there was something supernatural: that rests upon his word, and there it remains.'

The gentlewoman

Richard Baxter, in *The Certainty of the World of Spirits* (1691), has the following story.

'Mr *Franklin* is a Minister of the Church of *England*, and was then [1661] Minister of a Town in the Isle of *Ely*, and upon this Account which I shall tell you, removed to *Wood-Rising* in this County. This Man had a Child, to which a Spirit often appeared at his Father's House; and grew so bold and free, as very ordinarily to come in whilst Company was in the House, and *Franklin* in the Room, and sit down by the Boy. At due Years, about the Year 1661, he was bound an Apprentice to a Barber in Cambridge (or at least with him as a Probationer). One Night the Spirit appeared to him in the usual Habit of a Gentlewoman, and would have persuaded him to go home again, asking him what he did there etcetera. The Boy, after some Treaty [entreaty], replied, He would not go. Upon which, he received a great Blow on the Ear, and grew very ill, but rose. Being and continuing ill, his Master presently horseth, and rides to acquaint his Father. In the Forenoon of that day, the Boy sitting by the Kitchin-fire, his Mistress being by, he suddenly cries out, *O Mistress! Look: There's the Gentlewoman.* The Woman turns to look, sees nothing: but while her Head was turned, hears a Noise as of a great Box on the Ear; turns, sees the Boy bending down his Neck, and he presently died. About the same Hour, so near as they could guess, the Master was sitting at Dinner in the Isle of Ely, with the Father: the Appearance of a Gentlewoman comes in, looking angrily, taking a Turn or two, disappeared.

'Thus I remember the Story came, in three Days after it was done, to me. Mr *Cooper* this afternoon confirms it, as heard by him from Mr *Franklin* himself. Adding, the poor Man was so affected, that he seemed almost stupid.'

The old press

THE FOLLOWING NARRATIVE APPEARED IN A COPY OF *NOTES AND QUERIES* (1904). The narrator was there described as 'a well-informed young lady' of common sense and judgement.

'A short time ago I went with a friend to pay a visit to a family in the neighbourhood of Lancaster. We were very cordially received at Bair Hall by the hostess, who assigned to our use a spacious bedroom with old-fashioned furniture, and we noticed particularly an old press. My companion and myself retired to bed, and enjoyed a good night's rest. I happened to awaken at about five o'clock, it being a bright summer's morning, broad daylight, and to my great surprise saw distinctly within a few feet of the old-fashioned bed, an old gentleman seated in an arm-chair, earnestly gazing at me with a pleasant expression of countenance.

'I was not alarmed, but surprised, as I had locked the door when I went to bed, and, considering it a mental delusion, I closed my eyes for a moment and looked again; in the interval the old gentleman had moved his chair, and placed its back against the chamber door; he was seated in it as before, and gazed at me with rather an amused expression. I turned round to look at my companion; she was fast asleep. I immediately awoke her, and requested her to look across the room at the door. She could see nothing; neither could I; the old gentleman had gone. When I told her what I had seen, she got out of bed in haste; we both quitted the room in great alarm, and went to the bedroom of our hostess, who admitted us, and there we remained until it was time to dress.

'This lady asked if we had opened the old press wardrobe; it appeared we had. "Oh," said she, "it is only James Bair, my uncle: he does not like anyone but myself to examine his ancient clothes or interfere with his press. He frequently joins me in the house, and some of the other members of the family also, but they don't like him. With me he often converses."

'I found if any of the rooms or closets were locked at night they were found open in the morning, and our hostess thought nothing of it.'

The shudder

This is the story of 'Mr T. Westwood' noted down from *Notes and Queries* by John H. Ingram at the end of the nineteenth century.

'In a lonely spot on the verge of Enfield Chase stands an old house, much beaten by wind and weather. It was inhabited when I knew it by two elderly people, maiden sisters, with whom I had some acquaintance, and who once invited me to dine with them, and meet a circle of local guests. I well remember my walk thither. It led me up a steep ascent of oak avenue, opening out at the top on what was called the "ridge road" of the Chase. It was the close of a splendid afternoon. On reaching my destination the sun had already dipped below the horizon, and the eastern front projected a black shadow at its foot.

'Having some changes to make to my attire, a servant led the way to an upper chamber, and left me. No sooner was he gone than I became conscious of a peculiar sound in the room – a sort of shuddering sound in the room, as of suppressed dread. It seemed close to me. I gave little heed to it at first, setting it down for the wind in the chimney, or a draught from the half-open door; but moving about the room I perceived that the sound moved with me. Whichever way

I turned it followed me. I went to the furthest extremity of the chamber – it was there also.

'Beginning to feel uneasy, and being quite unable to account for the singularity, I completed my toilet in haste, and descended to the drawing room, hoping I should thus leave the uncomfortable sound behind me; but not so. It was on the landing, on the stair, it went down with me, always the same sound of shuddering horror, faint, but audible, and always close at hand. Even at the dinner table, when the conversation flagged, I heard it unmistakably several times, and so near, that, if there was an entity connected with it, we were two on one chair. It seemed to be noticed by nobody else, but it ended by harassing and distressing me, and I was relieved to think that I had not to sleep in the house that night.

'At an early hour, several guests having far to go, the party broke up, and it was a satisfaction to me to breathe the fresh wholesome air of the night, and feel rid at last of my shuddering incubus.

'When I saw my hosts again, it was under another and unhaunted roof. On my telling them what had occurred to me, they smiled and said it was perfectly true, but added that they were so used to the sound that it had ceased to perturb them. Sometimes, they said, it would be quiet for weeks, at others it followed them from room to room, from floor to floor, pertinaciously, as it had followed me. They could give me no explanation of the phenomenon. It was a sound, no more, and quite harmless.

'Perhaps so. But of what strange horror, not ended with life but perpetuated in the limbo of invisible things, was that sound the exponent?'

The old saloon

An account in the weekly periodical, *All the Year Round*, in the winter of 1870, tells the story of a small ghost.

'Direct ocular evidence, or the strongest circumstantial evidence, being the rule in courts of law, nothing is hereafter stated on the warrant of the writer that would not be considered good legal evidence. The facts come direct from the witnesses themselves, and were by them repeated to the writer. The scene to which I invite the reader's attention is that of Combermere Abbey in Cheshire.

'The old part of this fine old mansion has been made into bedrooms and offices, not being in keeping with the splendour of modern requirements. Thus what was used to be called the "coved saloon" was first degraded into a nursery, and is now used as a bedroom. When the late Lord Cotton grew old, this room, in which he had played as a child, was occupied by his niece, Miss P., who before her marriage resided in the house. Lady Cotton's dressing room was only divided from the "coved saloon" by a short corridor.

'One evening Miss P. was alone, dressing for a very late dinner, and as she rose from her toilet-glass to get some articles of dress, she saw standing near her bed – a little iron one, placed out in the room away from the wall – the figure of a child dressed in a very quaint frock, with an odd little ruff around its neck. For some moments Miss P. stood and stared, wondering how this strange little creature could have entered her room. The full glare of the candle was upon its face and figure. As she stood looking at it, the child began to run round the bed in a wild distressed way, with a look of suffering on its little face.

'Miss P., still more and more surprised, walked up to the bed and stretched out her hand, when the child suddenly vanished, how or where she did not see, but apparently into the floor. She went at once to Lady Cotton's room, and enquired of her to whom the little girl could belong she had just seen in her room, expressing her belief that it was supernatural and describing her odd dress and troubled face.

'The ladies went down to dinner, for many guests were staying in the house. Lady Cotton thought and thought over this strange appearance. At last she remembered that Lord Cotton had told her that one of his earliest recollections was the grief he felt at the sudden death of a little sister of whom he was very fond, four years old. The two children had been playing together in the nursery – the same "coved saloon" – running round and round the bed overnight.

'In the morning, when he woke, he was told that she had died in the night, and he was taken by one of the nursery-maids to see her laid out on her little bed in the "coved saloon". The sheet placed over her was removed to show him her face. The horror he felt at the first sight of death made so vivid an impression that in extreme old age he still recalled it. The dress and face of the child as described by Miss P. agreed precisely with his remembrance of his sister. Both Lady Cotton and Miss P. related this to the writer.'

The Barby apparition

THE SMALL VILLAGE OF BARBY WAS, IN THE MIDDLE OF THE NINETEENTH century, a secluded place just seven miles from the town of Rugby. On 3 March 1851, a widow of sixty-seven named Mrs Webb died in one of the cottages there. She was in life parsimonious to the point of being mean. She seemed to be aware of her impending dissolution and, three hours before her death, she turned to her two nurses and told them that she would not survive the night. In that, she was proved to be correct.

About a month later the occupants of the cottage next to hers, Mrs Holding and her uncle, were astonished by the sound of loud thumps against the partition wall; the door of a cupboard in the same wall shook violently. These sounds were followed by the noises of doors being violently slammed, and furniture being dragged over the floor. This was odd enough, since every article of furniture had been removed after the funeral. Mrs Holding had keys to the next-door cottage and, on entering it, everything was quiet. These noises continued for several weeks, generally starting at two o'clock in the morning. The uproar was so great that Mrs Harding and her uncle would retire to bed as late as possible to give them the chance of sleeping through it.

On 9 April a family by the name of Accleton moved into Mrs Webb's cottage. Mr and Mrs Accleton themselves occupied the bedroom in which the old lady had died. The eldest child, a girl of ten, slept in a small bed in a corner close to her parents. One night, soon after they had entered possession of the cottage, Mrs Accleton was woken from sleep by a tremendous crash in the room below; it sounded as though all the chairs and tables had been collected together, and then thrown violently down upon the wooden floor. She thought that it was her husband coming home, drunk, and called out, 'Oh so you've come at last, I hear!' There was no reply. The noises continued for another two hours, but Mr Accleton did not return home until seven o'clock on the following morning. The same noises were subsequently heard every night, to a greater or lesser degree. Nothing in the affected rooms was ever disturbed.

Then, a few weeks later, at approximately two o'clock in the morning, the Accletons were woken by a shriek from their young daughter. She cried out, 'Mother! Mother! There's a woman standing by my bed, a-shaking her head at me!' Mrs Accleton tried to calm her by saying that it was only the cap and gown that she had laid by the bed. This convenient lie was not enough to calm the child. Two hours later the girl cried out again, 'Mother, mother! Here's that woman come again!' She described the apparition as tall, wearing a white cap and mottled gown. Mrs Webb, the deceased, was in fact five feet and eleven inches in height. It had woken the girl by turning the corner of the sheet over her face.

So Mrs Accleton brought the girl into her own bed, and there was no further disturbance that night. But the visits did not stop. On seven subsequent nights the apparition was observed by the young girl, but the girl was progressively less alarmed. She described it as surrounded by a 'brown light'. It stood erect, sometimes with its hands apparently folded, and stared at the girl with a firm manner.

It had a low laughing, or singing, voice and seemed to be striving to speak.

Mrs Accleton, in the absence of her husband on business, asked her mother to sleep with her in the same bed. One night, at two in the morning, she was disturbed by a sudden light in the room. Immediately she considered the possibility of the apparition. 'I said to myself,' she said later, 'the Lord's will be done. I never did her any harm. I will *look* at her.' And she saw her, standing erect at the foot of the bed and staring 'as firm and proud as if she were alive'. It moved towards her, and seemed to press upon the bolster of the bed as if wishing to speak. Then Mrs Accleton turned to her mother and roused her. 'There is Mrs Webb,' she said.

The mother replied, 'Lord help us, don't see it.' Then she pulled the sheets over her head.

There were other witnesses who slept in the same room. One neighbour, Mrs Radburn, was sleeping on the couch there when she was aroused by what she called a pressure on the elbow. Then she saw the figure of Mrs Webb standing between her and the window. Another neighbour became conscious of the presence of the apparition, and put her hand across her face. 'I "sleered" my eyes through the room, sir, and said to myself "*Old wench, you shan't know I'm a-seeing of you.*"' But she did see it. It was wearing a dark mottled gown and a double-bordered white cap. A light came from it that, according to the neighbour, 'filled my eyes with fire'. These were the circumstances of the Barby ghost. After approximately a year, the disturbances ceased.

Mother Leakey

An old woman, known universally in the Somerset town of Minehead as 'Mother Leakey', died in her bed in the autumn of 1634. She had a reputation for conviviality, but she did also seem to have a taste for the macabre. 'As pleasing as my company now is to you,' she is reported to have told some of her friends, 'you will not care to see and converse with me when I am dead, though I believe you may.' About six weeks after the funeral her daughter-in-law, Elizabeth Leakey, was disturbed by the sounds of tapping and knocking in her bedchamber. At a later legal hearing she testified that it 'went away like a Drove of Cattell'. A year later her young son, John, died of a 'languishinge disease' during the course of which he complained that he was restless 'because of his Grandmother'. He did not, however, claim that he had actually seen her.

But his mother did. In March 1636 she was going up to her bedchamber, carrying a book in her hand, when she observed the shape of her mother-in-law sitting in a chair and dressed in the clothes she wore in life. These were 'a black gown, a kerchief, and a white stomacher' that covered the dead woman's chest and bosom. She was so astonished at this apparition that 'she could not speake to it nor stirre'; it lingered for quarter of an hour, and then vanished. On 16 October of the same year the curate of the town, John Heathfield, paid a visit to the Leakey household. At approximately nine o'clock that evening the reverend 'went forth to make water' and, on returning to the house, he saw Mother Leakey standing before him; from the light of a candle in the kitchen he could 'see the shape of her face and very countenance'. He left the house 'much affrighted'.

He said nothing at the time, but revealed his experience to Elizabeth Leakey a few days later. She was not at all surprised; she told him that she had seen the phantasmal figure following him. Four weeks later at seven o'clock in the morning Elizabeth saw her mother-in-law once more, beside her husband's warehouse about three hundred yards from the main house. She did not see the face of the phantom figure on this occasion, but only 'her back partes'.

About the time of this apparition a maid, Elizabeth Fluellin, was visited. She had joined the family after Mother Leakey's death, so she did not recognise the unexpected stranger. She was leaving the parlour at eight in the morning when she saw the 'shape of a woman with a pale wrisled face standing before her, wearing a black gowne, a white stomacher of shagge and a Kercher on her hair to her seeminge'. The apparition vanished suddenly away.

There was a last and more elaborate appearance. Elizabeth Leakey was in one of the smaller bedchambers, with only enough room between the bed and the wall to enter or leave the room. She was about to go when she found the narrow way blocked by the shape of her mother-in-law. She particularly noted that the eyes of the apparition did not move. 'In the name of God,' she said, 'do me no hurt.'

'I cannot,' Mother Leakey replied, 'God is with thee.'

Elizabeth Fluellin, working in a downstairs room, subsequently testified that at this time she could hear the sound of voices. Some brief words were exchanged between them, at the conclusion of which Elizabeth Leakey asked if her mother-in-law were in heaven or hell. There was no reply. Mother Leakey never returned.

So great was the astonishment at the events in Minehead that a special 'county commission' of judges was established by the Privy Council in London. They examined the witnesses, among them Elizabeth Leakey and Elizabeth Fluellin, and believed that there were inconsistencies that rendered their testimony dubious. But the real causes for Mother Leakey's appearances were utterly opaque to them. They concluded that it was 'an Imposture devised and framed for some endes but what they were wee know not'. It remains, therefore, an intriguing episode.

The unfurnished rooms

AT THE END OF THE NINETEENTH CENTURY SOME VISITORS TO CARLISLE, a colonel and his family, were fortunate enough to find a furnished house in the city that was being rented at a remarkably low rate. They were told by others that 'no one liked to live in it', for cause or causes unknown, but they dismissed the rumours as idle and fanciful chatter. Indeed they were subject to no annoyance. Then, at the start of race week in Carlisle, they were expecting the company of certain friends.

The house was large, and there were two rooms within it that had been left unused and unfurnished during this period of their stay. Now, however, they were temporarily fitted up for the benefit of nurses and children. There, for that week, they were to sleep. There were heavy venetian blinds fixed to the window and one night a nurse was woken by the distinct sound of the blinds being pulled up and down with great strength and violence; this was repeated some twenty times. Since the fire had fallen low she could not see if the blinds had actually moved or not; so she remained trembling in a state of understandable fright and horror. Then presently she heard the sound of feet moving about the room as if several men were, in her words, 'moving about without stockings'. She was in such an agony of terror that she was reassured by the sudden cry of a nurse who slept in an adjacent bed — 'The Lord have mercy on us!' This second nurse then asked her companion if she had the courage to get out of bed and stir the fire, so that the room might be seen; she did so but in the light of the reviving fire there was no evidence of any disturbance. All was as before.

On another occasion the two nurses were sitting together in one of the previously unfurnished rooms, sewing, when they both distinctly heard someone counting money, with the chink of the pieces and the sound of each coin being laid down. The noise came from the inner room of the two but, on entering it, they found nobody there. On being acquainted with these events the colonel and his family decided to leave the house. It remained unoccupied for a long time.

The scratching

The following letter from John Caswell, the eighteenth-century Oxford mathematician, was found among the papers of Richard Bentley, a classical scholar and Master of Trinity College, Cambridge.

'Sir,

'When I was in London, April last, I fully intended to have waited upon you again, but cold and lameness seized me next day: the cold took away my voice, and the other my power of walking; so I presently took coach for Oxford. I am much your debtor; and in particular for your good intentions in relation to Mr D. though that, as it has proved, would not have turned to my advantage: however, I am obliged to you upon that and other accounts, and, if I had opportunity to show it, you should find how much I am your faithful servant. I have sent you enclosed a relation of an apparition: the story I had from two persons, who each had it from the author, and yet their accounts somewhat varied and, passing through more mouths, have varied still more; therefore I got a friend to bring me to the author's, at a chamber, where I wrote it down from the author's mouth; after which I read it to him, and gave him another copy. He said he could swear to the truth of it, as far as he is concerned; he is the curate of Warblington, bachelor of arts of Trinity College, in Oxford, about six years' standing in the university: I hear no ill report of his behaviour here; he is now gone to his curacy; he has promised to send up the hands of the tenant and his man, who is a smith by trade, and the farmer's men, as far as they are concerned. Mr Brinton, the rector, would have him say nothing of the story: for that he can get no tenant, although he has offered the house for ten pounds a year less. Mr P., the former incumbent, whom the apparition represented, was a man of very ill report, supposed to have got children of his maid and to have murdered them; but I advised the curate to say nothing himself of this last part of P. but leave that to the parishioners who knew him. Those who knew this P. say he had exactly such a gown, and that he used to whistle.

    'Yours,

    'J. CASWELL.'

NARRATIVE

At Warblington, near Havant, in Hampshire, within six miles of Portsmouth, in the parsonage house, dwelt Thomas Perse, the tenant, with his wife and a child, a man-servant, Thomas, and a maid-servant. About the beginning of 1695, on a Monday, about nine or ten at night, all being in bed, except the maid with the child, the maid, being in the kitchen and having raked up the fire, took a candle in one hand and the child in the other arm and, turning about, saw one in a black gown walking through the room, and thence out of the door into the orchard. Upon this the maid, hasting up stairs, having covered but two steps, cried out; on which the master and mistress ran down, found the candle in her hand, she grasping the child around the neck with the other arm: she told them the reason of her crying out. She would not that night tarry in the house, but removed to another, belonging to one Henry Salter, farmer, where she cried out all the night, from the terror she was in; and she could not be persuaded to go any more to the house, on any terms.

On the morrow (Tuesday) the tenant's wife came to me, lodging then at Havant, to desire my advice, and have consult with some friends about it; I told her I thought it was a flam, and that they had a mind to abuse Mr Brereton, the rector, whose house it was: I told her I would come up, and sit up or lie there, as she pleased; for then, as to all stories of ghosts or apparitions, I was an infidel. I went thither, and sat up the Tuesday night, with the tenant and the man-servant; about twelve or one o'clock I searched all the rooms in the house, to see if any body was hid there to impose upon me. At last we came to a lumber room: there, I smiling, told the tenant that was with me that I would call for the apparition and oblige him to come. The tenant then seemed to be afraid, but I told him I would defend him from harm, and then I repeated 'Barbara, celarent Darii etc.' On this the tenant's countenance changed, so that he was ready to drop down with fear; and I told him I perceived he was afraid, and I would prevent its coming, and repeated – 'Baralipton etc.'; then he recovered his spirits pretty well, and we left the room and went down into the kitchen, where we were before, and sat up there the remaining part of the night, and had no manner of disturbance.

Thursday night the tenant and I lay together in one room, and the man in another room; and he saw something walk along in a black gown, and place itself against a window, and there stood for some time, and then walked off. Friday morning, the man relating this, I asked him why he did not call me, and I told him I thought that was a trick or flam; he told me the reason he did not call me was that he was not able to speak or move. Sunday night I lay by myself in one room (not that where the man saw the apparition), and the tenant and the man in one bed in another room; and, betwixt twelve and two, the man heard something walk in their room at the bed's foot, and whistling very well; and at last it came to the bed's side, drew the curtain, and looked on them; after some time it moved off; then the man called to me, desired me to come, for that there was something in the room that went about whistling. I asked him whether he had any light, or could strike one; he told me, no. Then I leaped out of bed and, not staying to put on my clothes, went out of my room and along a gallery to the door, which I found locked or bolted; I desired him to unlock the door, for that I could not get in; then he got out of bed and opened the door, which was near, and went immediately again to bed.

I went in three or four steps; and, it being a moonshine night, I saw the apparition move from the bedside, and clap up against the wall that divided their room and mine. I went and stood directly against it, within my arm's length of it, and asked it in the name of God what it was that made it come disturbing of us. I stood some time, expecting an answer, and, receiving none, thinking it might be some fellow hid in the room to fright me, I put out my arm to feel it, and my hand seemingly went through the body of it, and felt no manner of substance till it came to the wall; then I drew back my hand, and still it was in the same place. Till now I had not the least fear, and even now had very little.

Then I adjured it to tell me what it was: when I had said those words it, keeping its back against the wall, moved gently along towards the door; I followed it, and it, going out at the door, turned its back towards me; it went a little along the gallery, and it disappeared where there was no corner for it to turn, and before it came to the end of the gallery where were the stairs. Then I found myself very cold from my feet as high as my middle, though I was not in great fear: I went into the bed betwixt the tenant and his man, and they complained of my being exceeding cold. The tenant's man leaned over his master in the bed, and saw me stretch out my hand towards the apparition, and heard me speak the words; the tenant also heard the words.

The apparition seemed to have a morning gown of a darkish colour, no hat nor cap, short black hair, a thin meagre visage, of a pale swarthy colour; seemed to be of about five and forty or fifty years of age; the eyes half shut, the arms hanging down, the hands visible beneath the sleeve; of a middle stature. I related this description to Mr John Lardner, rector of Havant, and to Major Batten, of Langstone, in Havant parish; they both said that the description agreed very well to Mr P. a former rector of the place, who had been dead for twenty years. Upon this the tenant and his wife left the place, which has remained void ever since.

The Monday after last Michaelmas day, a man of Chodson, in Warwickshire, having been at Havant fair, passed by the aforesaid parsonage house about nine or ten at night, and saw a light in most of the rooms of the house. His pathway being close by the house he, wondering at the light, looked into the kitchen window, and saw only a light; but, turning himself to go away, he saw the appearance of a man in a long gown; he made haste away; the apparition followed him over a piece of glebe land of several acres, to a lane which he crossed, and over a little meadow; then over another lane to some pales, which belong to farmer Henry Salter, my landlord, near a barn, in which were some of the farmer's men and others. This man went into the barn, and told them how he was frightened and followed from the parsonage house by an apparition, which they might see standing against the pales if they went out; they went out and saw it scratch against the pales and make a hideous noise; it stood there some time, and then disappeared; their description agrees with what I saw.

This last account I had from the man himself, and also from the farmer's men.

THOMAS WILKINS,
Curate of Warblington
December 11, 1695

The restless suicide

The following narrative was supplied to the Reverend Frederick George Lee, the author of *Glimpses in the Twilight* (1884), by a clergyman in the diocese of Rochester.

'I had been invited to go to a clerical conference in the south of England where, as I was given to understand, a few leading clergy were to assemble to discuss several very practical questions relating to their work and office. The conference was to last three days, but unanticipated circumstances prevented my going until the second day. The clergyman at whose house the conference was to be held was a stranger to me, though some correspondence had passed between us. On reaching my destination I received a very cordial welcome from my host. His wife directed that I should be shown to a bedroom, and apologised for its size, its northern aspect, and the scantiness of its furniture, remarking that it was only used when the house was quite full.

'I was just in time to attend the latter part of the second day's conference, after which we dined, and in due course I went to bed. In the middle of the night I awoke much oppressed with the feeling that something like a large animal appeared to be lying on my chest, and that I had a difficulty in breathing.

'Arousing myself at once, I sat up in the bed, recovering my breath immediately; when, in the dimness of the gloom, I thought I saw the bent figure of a person, clothed in a long dressing gown or similarly flowing garment, slowly gliding backwards and forwards around the room.

'Upon this, I struck a light and lit the candle by my bedside. Even in the glare of the candle I still continued to see the gliding shadowy form moving as before, though it was obscure in outline and dim in colour. It soon began to fade away, though its motion was continued. My curiosity being greatly excited, I kept the light burning for at least half an hour; but the figure did not reappear. I lay awake a little unnerved until the morning began to dawn; and then, being weary, fell asleep.

'When I went down to breakfast, somewhat late, the lady of the house, noticing that I was looking pale and fatigued – as indeed was the case – enquired, with some obvious nervousness, if I had slept comfortably. I hesitatingly replied in the negative; but without giving the why and the wherefore, or appearing to be at all disconcerted. Later in the day, when the subject was again mentioned by her, I learnt that a tradition existed that the man-servant of the previous rector had committed suicide in that room – which, as a rule, was never used; and that many persons had seen the indistinct form of the restless apparition gliding backwards and forwards round the large bedstead. At other times a constant tramping across the floor of the room was heard; and reports existed that piercing shrieks sometimes came therefrom in the stillness of the night.'

Mrs M—

AN OFFICER IN THE ENGLISH ARMY, OF THE MID-NINETEENTH CENTURY, has left a record of his interrogation of two soldiers concerning a phenomenon that occurred in the garrison hospital of his regiment. It was reprinted in Catherine Crowe's *The Night Side of Nature* (1852). These are his words.

'About the month of August my attention was requested by the schoolmaster-sergeant, a man of considerable worth, and highly esteemed by the whole corps, to an event which had occurred in the garrison hospital. Having heard his recital which, from the serious earnestness with which he made it, challenged attention, I resolved to investigate the matter; and having communicated the circumstances to a friend, we both repaired to the hospital for the purposes of inquiry.

'There were two patients to be examined − both men of good character, and neither of them suffering from any disorder affecting the brain; the one was under treatment for consumptive symptoms, and the other for an ulcerated leg: and they were both in the prime of life.

'Having received a confirmation of the schoolmaster's statement from the hospital-sergeant, also a very respectable and trustworthy man, I sent for the patient principally concerned, and desired him to state what he had seen and heard, warning him at the same time that it was my intention to take down his deposition, and that it behoved him to be very careful, as possible serious steps might be taken for the purpose of discovering whether an imposition had been practised in the wards of the hospital – a crime for which, as he was well aware, a very severe penalty would be inflicted. He then proceeded to relate the circumstances which I took down as follows.

'"It was late Tuesday night, somewhere between eleven and twelve, when all of us were in bed, and all lights out except the rush-light that was allowed for the man with the fever, when I was awoke by feeling a weight upon my feet, and at the same moment, as I was drawing up my legs, Private W——, who lies in the cot opposite mine, called out, 'I say, Q——, there's somebody sitting upon your legs!' – and as I looked to the bottom of the bed, I saw someone get up from it, and then come round and stand over me, in the passage between my cot and the next. I felt somewhat alarmed, for the last few nights the ward had been disturbed by sounds as of a heavy foot walking up and down; and as nobody could be seen, it was beginning to be supposed among us that it was haunted, and fancying this that came up to my bed's head might be the ghost I called out, 'Who are you and what do you want?'

'"The figure then, leaning with one hand on the wall, over my head, and, stooping down, said in my ear, 'I am Mrs M——'; and I could then distinguish that she was dressed in a flannel gown, edged with black riband, exactly similar to a set of grave-clothes in which I had assisted to clothe her corpse, when her death took place a year previously.

'"The voice, however, was not like Mrs M——'s nor like anybody else's, yet it was very distinct, and seemed somehow to sing through my head. I could see nothing of a face beyond a darkish colour about the head, and it appeared to me that I could see through her body against the window glasses.

'"Although I felt very uncomfortable I asked her what she wanted. She replied, 'I am Mrs M——, and I wish you to write to him that was my husband and tell him . . .'

'"I am not, sir," said Corporal Q——, "at liberty to mention to anybody what she told me, except to her husband. He is at the depot in Ireland, and I have written and told him. She made me promise not to tell anyone else. After I had promised secrecy, she told me something of a matter that convinced me I was talking to a spirit, for it related to what only I and Mrs M—— knew, and no one living could know anything whatever of the matter; and if I was now speaking my last words on earth I say solemnly that it was Mrs M——'s spirit that spoke to me then, and no one else. After promising me that if I complied with her request, she would not trouble me or the ward again, she went from my bed towards the fireplace, and with her hands she kept feeling about the wall over the mantelpiece. After a while she came towards me again; and while my eyes were upon her, she somehow disappeared from my sight altogether, and then I was left alone.

'"It was then that I felt faint-like, and a cold sweat broke out over me; but I did not faint, and after a time I got better, and gradually I went off to sleep."

'After closely cross-questioning Corporal Q——, and endeavouring without success to reason him out of his belief in the ghostly character of his visitor, I read over to him what I had written, and then, dismissing him, sent for the other patient.

'After cautioning him, as I had done the first, I proceeded to take down his statement, which was made with every appearance of good faith and sincerity:—

'"I was lying awake," said he, "last Tuesday night, when I saw someone sitting on Corporal Q—'s bed. There was so little light in the ward, that I could not make out who it was, and the figure looked so strange that I got alarmed, and felt quite sick. I called out to Corporal Q— that there was somebody sitting upon his bed, and then the figure got up; and as I did not know but it might be coming to me, I got so much alarmed, that being but weakly [this was the consumptive man], I fell back and I believe I fainted away. When I got round again, I saw the figure standing and apparently talking to the corporal, placing one hand against the wall and stooping down. I could not, however, hear any voice; and being still much alarmed, I put my head under the clothes for a considerable time. When I looked up again I could see only Corporal Q—, sitting up in bed alone, and he said that he had seen a ghost; and I told him I had also seen it. After a time he got up and gave me a drink of water, for I was very faint. Some of the other patients being disturbed by our talking, they bade us be quiet, and after some time I got to sleep. The ward has not been disturbed since."

'The man was then cross-questioned; but his testimony remaining quite unshaken, he was dismissed, and the hospital-sergeant was interrogated with regard to the possibility of a trick having been practised. He asserted, however, that this was impossible; and, certainly, from my own knowledge of the hospital regulations, and the habits of the patients, I should say that a practical joke of this nature was too serious a thing to have been attempted by anybody, especially as there were patients in the ward very ill at the time and one very near his end. The punishments would have been extremely severe, and discovery almost certain, since everybody would have been adverse to the delinquent.

'The investigation that ensued was a very brief one, it being found that there was nothing more to be elicited; and the affair terminated with the supposition that the two men had been dreaming. Nevertheless, six months afterward, on being interrogated, their evidence and their conviction were as clear as at first, and they declared themselves ready at any time to repeat their statements upon oath.'

There ends the story of the two soldiers in the hospital ward. There are perhaps reasons for scepticism. Why did Mrs M— not appear to her husband directly rather than to this intermediary? Why did she appear only on this particular night, the noise of a heavy footfall being heard on previous nights? But there are small details that suggest the veracity of the two witnesses – the ward being dark, with all lights out 'except the rush-light that was allowed for the man with the fever'. Then there is the strange account of how the spirit or apparition 'kept feeling about the wall over the mantelpiece'. There is also the second soldier's description of the spirit 'placing one hand against the wall and stooping down'. Could the presence of a man 'near to his end', or the severe illnesses of many other patients, have helped to create this manifestation? There are many accounts of ghosts in hospitals.

The drunkard

RICHARD BAXTER, IN *THE CERTAINTY OF THE WORLD OF SPIRITS* (1691), has the following anecdote.

'There is now in London an understanding, sober, pious Man, oft one of my Hearers who hath an elder Brother, a Gentleman of considerable Rank, who having formerly seemed pious, of late Years doth oft fall into the Sin of Drunkenness: He oft lodgeth long together here, in his Brother's House: And whenever he is drunken, and hath slept himself sober, some thing knocks at his Bed's Head, as if one knock'd on a Wainscot; when they remove his Bed, it followeth him: Beside lowd Noises on other parts where he is, that all the House heareth. They have oft watch'd, and kept his Hands, lest he should do it himself. His Brother hath oft told it me, and brought his Wife (a discreet Woman) to attest it: who averreth moreover, that as she watched him, she hath seen his Shoes under the Bed taken up, and nothing visible touch them. They brought to me the Man himself, and when we ask him how he dare so sin again, after such a Warning, he hath no Excuse. But being Persons of Quality, for some special Reason of Worldly Interest, I must not name him.'

At the end of the hall

IN AUGUST 1912 THE MARQUIS OF HUNTINGTON, LATER TO BECOME THE eighth Duke of Devonshire, was staying with some companions at Bolton Hall, a grand house situated three miles north of Skipton in Yorkshire. He was sleeping in the rectory next door to the house itself. His companions included the Duke of Devonshire, Lord Desborough, and the reigning monarch King George V. The first document in the case consists of a statement made by the Marquis of Huntington, to which the signatures of the three eminent gentlemen were appended as witnesses.

'On Sunday, 18 August 1912, on going up to my room at the rectory, at 11.15 p.m., I distinctly saw a figure standing at the door. It was dressed in non-descript clothes and was more or less clean-shaven. I was at the top of the staircase, looking down the passage in which mine was the end room. I went downstairs again and fetched another light, but on going up again the figure had disappeared.

'The ghost had been the subject of a conversation that

evening at which I had not been present, and I was not thinking of it.'

(Signed) Hartington

The second document is a letter from the Marquis of Huntington's mother to Lady Halifax.

'Will you tell Lord Halifax that Eddy [the Marquis of Huntington] will send him an account of his ghost? He seems to be the same man who was seen two or three times by the vicar, but the vicar's ghost wore a brown dress and Eddy declared this man's was dark grey or black. Eddy's ghost had a round face – no beard, but what he described as a rough face. When we asked the vicar afterwards if his ghost had a beard he said, "no", but that he looked as if he had not shaved for four or five days, and his face was very round.'

The third letter was sent to Lord Halifax by the Marquis of Huntington himself.

'I saw the ghost standing in the door of my room looking not at, but past, me at 11.15 p.m. on Sunday August 18. I was sleeping at the rectory and I saw him when I turned left-handed from the stairs, which are in three flights, and looked down the passage some 11 yards long, at the end of which is the door of my room. While I was going up the last flight, which consists only of six steps, I thought someone was there but attached no importance to this, as the rector often met me on the stairs.

'I thought at once that it was the ghost, but was not

frightened of him until afterwards. He was below the middle height and seemed to be a man of sixty-five or so. His face was unusually round, or, rather, broad in proportion to its length, and was very heavily lined and wrinkled. The eyes were bright and the face might have been that of an old woman, but for the fact that there was about a week's growth of greyish stubble on the chin. There was a hood over the head and he was dressed in a long garment like a dressing gown. The hood and the shoulders seemed to be grey, but lower down the colour was black or brown. The light was behind me and I had a candle in my hand, so that his head and shoulders were fairly brightly lighted, while lower down he was in shadow. The phantom was not at all transparent, but solid and real.'

The wall of the room, in which the marquis slept, was in fact part of the wall of an old priory that had been erected on this site. The vicar to whom the Marquis of Huntington's mother alludes, Reverend Mr MacNabb, saw the phenomenon only once. It was standing in the same position where it was seen by the marquis, and seemed so real that the vicar challenged him for trespassing. Then it disappeared. It has apparently been seen by others in more recent years.

The chattering voices

MR JAMES WAYLAND OF BATH COMMUNICATED THE FOLLOWING NARRATIVE to the Reverend Frederick George Lee who repeated it in his *Glimpses in the Twilight* (1884).

'My father purchased the freehold of a small and comfortable house, called "Hotwells", with two acres of land, near Bristol, about the year 1829. It stood quite alone – away from the village, but not far from the village church; and there he intended to settle, having quitted his old house in London, and given up his profession (the legal). He thought the place quite a bargain. It had been dilapidated, but the owner had covenanted to put everything into repair, on condition of recovering a fair amount for the absolute freehold. This was paid, and everything settled, in the spring of 1831.

'My father, with my youngest sister, a man-servant and two maid-servants, went to reside there in April; when, within a fortnight, both the female servants gave notice to leave. The house, they maintained, was haunted by two animals – a large ape, and a huge black dog. One or the other of these creatures appeared in several of the rooms, and was constantly passing them in the passages and on the stairs; while the strange noises – which were heard elsewhere – alarmed them greatly. In an empty attic the most frightful sounds were heard, as of people being strangled; and sometimes noises and shouts, as of twenty or thirty persons being beaten severely, came from the court-yard. When they went to investigate the cause of such noises, nothing was seen, nothing heard. The yard was then as still and silent as the grave, and no explanation of the mystery was forthcoming.

'On several nights some of the villagers were induced to keep watch; but they would only do so with lights and lanterns, and in a considerable company. On these occasions the noises then were only heard in the attics; but, about midnight, the apparitions of the ape and the black dog appeared in the courtyard and were seen by five persons at once. They seemed to come up through a closed grating from a large cellar underneath an outhouse, and to rush out into the darkness beyond the gates of the enclosure. At least a dozen times these apparitions were seen by the tenants and the villagers, though my father and the man-servant (who had both heard strange enough noises) had never seen anything.

'Early in November, 1831, however, when he had changed servants two or three times, he was awaked in the middle of the night by a frightful scream which came, or seemed to come, from the roof of the house: and noises simultaneously reached him which seemed as if twenty or thirty chattering workmen were removing the tiles, and flinging them down as fast as possible into the garden below. He hastily got up, assumed part of his clothes and dressing gown and, summoning the man-servant, went down with him to the front door, armed with a brace of loaded pistols and a blunderbuss. They expected to find thieves, or a body of lunatics, or Chartist rioters on an errand of destruction. But on opening the door and making examination, not a soul was to be seen – not a sound heard. None of the tiles had been removed; while the garden was perfectly still and deserted.

'Similar occurrences, differing somewhat in detail, took place again and again. My father, who was a most unimaginative and prosaic man, came to the distinct conclusion that the house was haunted – as certainly seems to have been the case – and got rid of it to a retired Bristol tradesman in 1832.

'He in turn, I am told, found his life unbearable there, was unable to dispose of it, and so turned it into three cottages. But even the cottagers – having similar experiences – refused to live there: the spot got a bad reputation; the windows of the untenanted place were broken; the premises in due course went to ruin, and in a few years were pulled down.'

The little girl

THE FOLLOWING NARRATIVE APPEARED IN *NOTES AND QUERIES* OF MARCH 1880. It came from the pen of 'a young lady'.

'What I am going to relate happened to myself while staying with some north country cousins, last July, at their house in Yorkshire. I had spent a few days there in the summer of the previous year, but without then hearing or seeing anything out of the common. On my second visit, arriving early in the afternoon, I went out boating with some of the family, spent a very jolly evening, and finally went to bed, a little tired perhaps with the day's work, but not the least nervous. I slept soundly until between three and four, just when the day was beginning to break. I had been awake for a short time when suddenly the door of my bedroom opened, and shut again rather quickly. I fancied it might be one of the servants and called out, "Come in!"

'After a short time the door opened again, but no one came in – at least no one I could see. Almost at the same time as the door opened for the second time, I was a little startled by the rustling of some curtains belonging to a hanging wardrobe that stood by the side of the bed; the rustling continued, and I was seized with the most uncomfortable feeling, not exactly of fright, but a strange unearthly sensation that I was not alone.

'I had had that feeling for some minutes, when I saw at the foot of the bed a child, about seven or nine years old. The child seemed as if it were on the bed, and came gliding towards me as I lay. It was the figure of a little girl in her nightdress — a little girl with dark hair and a very white face. I tried to speak to her but could not. She came slowly on up to the top of the bed, and I then saw her face clearly. She seemed in great trouble; her hands were clasped and her eyes were turned up with a look of entreaty, an almost agonised look. Then, slowly unclasping her hands, she touched me on the shoulder. The hand felt icy cold, and while I strove to speak she was gone.

'I felt more frightened after the child was gone than before, and began to be very anxious for the time when the servant would make her appearance. Whether I slept again or not, I hardly know. But by the time the servant did come, I had almost persuaded myself that the whole affair was nothing but a very vivid nightmare. However, when I came down to breakfast, there were many remarks made about my not looking well — it was observed that I was pale. In answer I told my cousins that I had had a most vivid nightmare, and I remarked if I was a believer in ghosts I should imagine I had seen one. Nothing more was said at the time upon the subject, except that my host, who was a doctor, observed that I had better not sleep in the room again, at any rate not alone.

'So the following night one of my cousins slept in the same room with me. Neither one of us saw or heard anything out of the way during that night or the early morning. That being the case, I persuaded myself that what I had seen had been only imagination and, much against everyone's expressed wish, I insisted the next night on sleeping in the room again, and alone. Accordingly, having retired again to the same room, I was kneeling down at the bedside to say my prayers, when exactly the same dread as before came over me. The curtains of the wardrobe swayed about, and I had the same sensation as previously – that I was not alone. I felt too frightened to stir when, luckily for me, one of my cousins came in for something which she had left. On looking at me she exclaimed, "Have you seen anything?" I said, "No," but told her how I felt and, without much persuasion being necessary, I left the room with her and never returned to it. When my hostess learned what had happened (which she did immediately) she told me I must not sleep in that room again, as the nightmare had made such an impression on me; I should imagine (she said) all sorts of things and make myself quite ill. I went to another room, and during the rest of my visit (a week) I was not troubled by the reappearance of the little girl.

'On leaving, my cousin, the eldest daughter of the doctor, went on a visit with me to an uncle of mine in the same county. We stayed there for about a fortnight, and during the time the "little girl" was alluded to only as my "nightmare".

'In this I found afterwards there was a little reticence, for, just before leaving my uncle's, my cousin said to me, "I must tell you something I have been longing to tell you ever since I left home. But my father desired me not to tell you as, not being very strong, you might be too frightened. Your nightmare was not a nightmare at all, but the apparition of a little girl!" She then went on to tell me that this "little girl" had been seen three times before, by three different members of the family; but as this was some nine or ten years since, they almost ceased to think anything about it until I related my experiences on the morning after the first night of my second visit.

'My cousin further went on to tell me that her younger sister while in bed had one morning, about daybreak, to her great surprise, seen a little girl with dark hair, standing with her back to her, looking out of the window. She took this figure for her little sister, and spoke to it. The child not replying, or moving from her position, she called out to it, "It's no use standing like that; I know you. You can't play tricks with me." On looking round, however, she saw that her little sister, the one she thought she was addressing, and who was sleeping with her, had not moved from the bed.

'Almost at the same time the child passed from the window into the room of my cousin's sister, A——, and the latter, as she afterwards declared, distinctly saw the figure of a child with dark hair standing by the side of a table in her room. She spoke to it, and it instantly disappeared. The "little girl" was subsequently again seen, for the last time before I saw it, by my cousin's father Dr H——. It was in the early daylight of a summer's morning, and he was going upstairs to his room, having just returned from a professional visit. On this occasion he saw the same child (he noticed its dark hair) running up the stairs immediately before him, until it reached his room and entered it. When he got into the room it was gone.

'Thus the apparition has been seen three times by the family, and once by me. I am the only one, however, that has seen its face. It has, also, never been seen twice in the same room by anyone else.'

House guests

THERE ARE SOME ODD OR DISCONCERTING HOUSE PHANTOMS. THERE WAS a ghost in one of the eighteenth-century houses of Park Street in Windsor. It took the form of footsteps walking across the bedroom at night. A lady living in the house reported that 'I never saw anyone, but I continued to hear the footsteps. They went diagonally across the room, from an alcove beside the bed across to the far wall where they stopped. Somehow, I was never frightened . . . One day one of my children referred casually to the "nice old man who comes in to say good night".' The child was three years old and, when asked to describe the old man, replied, 'He's like Father Christmas. Only he's wearing burnt paper.'

There was a ghost in the house of a baker, near Stoney Middleton in Derbyshire in the nineteenth century, who made holes in the loaves of bread – 'so large that the loaves could not be sold'. In the same century a phantom was sometimes seen at Glowrowram near Chester-le-Street. When approached, 'the figure would fall down and spread out like a sheet, or rather like a great pack of white wool'. In the nineteenth century, in a house reputed to be haunted, some children told their mother that they had been running after 'such a queer thing in the cellar; it was like a goat and not like a goat; but it seemed to be like a shadow'. In 1661 there was an apparition that had a plaster on its face 'as broad as half a crown'. In the twentieth century, a blue eye was seen by mother and child peering through a knot-hole in a wooden floorboard.

The wandering ghost

The woman in the field

Here is an account from the pen of the Reverend Ruddle, minister and schoolteacher in the parish of Launceston in Cornwall, reprinted by T. M. Jarvis in *Accredited Ghost Stories* (1823).

'In the beginning of the year 1665 a disease happened in this town of Launceston, and some of my scholars died of it. Among others who fell under its malignity was John Elliott, the eldest son of Edward Treberse Esquire, a stripling of about sixteen years of age, but of uncommon parts and ingenuity. At his own particular request I preached at the funeral, which happened on the 20th day of June 1665. In my discourse I spoke some words in commendation of the young gentleman.

'The funeral rites being over, I was no sooner come out of the church, but I found myself most courteously accosted by an old gentleman; and with an unusual importunity, almost forced against my humour, to see his house that night. I got loose for that time, but was constrained to leave a promise behind me, to wait upon him at his own house the Monday following. This then seemed to satisfy but, before Monday came, I had a new message to request me that,

85

if it were possible, I would be there the Sunday. The second attempt I resisted, by answering that it was against my convenience, and the duty which mine own people expected from me. Yet was not the gentleman at rest, for he sent me another letter the Saturday by no means to fail the Monday, and so to order my business as to spend with him two or three days at least. I was indeed startled at so much eagerness.

'On the Monday I went and paid my promised devoir, and met with entertainment as free and plentiful as the invitation was importunate. There also, I found a neighbouring minister, who pretended to call in accidentally, but by the sequel I suppose it otherwise. After dinner this brother of the coat undertook to show me the gardens where, as we were walking, he gave me the first discovery of what was intended in all this treat and compliment.

'First he began to inform me of the infelicity of the family in general, and then gave instance in the youngest son. He related what a hopeful sprightly lad he lately was, and how melancholy and sottish he was now grown. Then did he with much passion lament that his ill-humour should so incredibly subdue his reason; (saith he) the poor boy believes himself to be haunted with ghosts, and is confident that he meets with an evil spirit in a certain field about half a mile from this place, as often as he goes that way to school.

'In the midst of our discourse the old gentleman and his lady (as observing their cue most exactly) came up to us. Upon their approach, and pointing me to the arbour, the parson renews the relation to me and they (the parents of the youth) confirmed what he said, and added many minute circumstances in a long narrative of the whole: in fine they all desired my thoughts and advice in the affair.

'I answered that the thing which the youth reported to them was strange, yet not incredible, and that I knew not then what to think or say of it; but if the lad would be free to me in talk, and trust me with his counsels, I had hopes to give them a better account of my opinion the next day.'

So the boy confers with the Reverend Ruddle and told him the following story.

'This woman, which appears to me, lived a neighbour here to my father, and died about eight years since; her name Dorothy Dingley, of such a stature, such age, and such complexion. She never speaks to me, but passes by hastily, and always leaves the footpath to me, and she commonly meets me twice or three times in the breadth of the field.

'It was about two months before I took any notice of it, and though the shape of the face was in my memory, yet I could not recall the name of the person: but without more thoughtfulness I did suppose that it was some woman who lived thereabout, and had frequent occasion that way. Nor did I imagine anything to the contrary, before she began to meet me constantly morning and evening, and always in the same field, and sometimes twice or thrice in the breadth of it.

'The first time I took notice of her was about a year since; and when I first began to suspect and believe it was a ghost, I had courage enough not to be afraid; but kept it to myself a good while, and only wondered very much at it. I did often speak to it, but never had a word in answer. Then I changed my way and went to school the under horse road, and then she always met me in the narrow lane, between the Quarry Park and the Nursery, which was worse.

'At length I began to be terrified of it, and prayed continually that God would either free me from it or let me know the meaning of it. Night and day, sleeping and waking, the shape was ever running in my mind. Thus by degrees I grew very pensive, insomuch that it was taken notice of by all our family; whereupon being urged to it,

I told my brother William of it, and he privately acquainted my father and mother, and they kept it to themselves for some time. The success of this discovery was only this: they did sometimes laugh at me, sometimes chide me, but still commanded me to keep my school and put such fopperies out of my head.

'I did accordingly go to school often, but always met the woman in the way.'

After listening to the boy's tale, the clergyman agreed to go with him at six o'clock on the following morning to the place where he had seen the phantom. They were to do so secretly, without telling the boys' parents of their mission. Reverend Ruddle continues his story.

'The next morning, before five o'clock, the lad was in my chamber, and very brisk; I arose and went with him. The field he led me to I guessed to be twenty acres, in an open country, and about three furlongs from any house. We went into the field, and had not gone above a third part, before the spectrum, in the shape of a woman, with all the circumstances he had described to me the day before (as much as the suddenness of its appearance and evanition would permit me to discover), met us and passed by. I was a little surprised at it, and though I had taken up a firm resolution to speak to it, yet I had not the power, nor indeed durst I look back, yet I took care not to show any fear to my pupil and guide; and therefore only telling him that I was satisfied as to the truth of his complaint, we walked to the end of the field, and returned, nor did the ghost meet us at that time above once.

'I perceived in the young man a kind of boldness mixed with astonishment; the first caused by my presence, and the proof he had given of his own relation, and the other by the sight of his persecutor. In short, we went home: I somewhat puzzled, he much animated.'

On their return Reverend Ruddle told the boy's mother that his evidence was 'not to be slighted, nor altogether discredited' and warned her not to mention the matter to anyone in the neighbourhood. He then returned to his own home, where much business awaited him, and had no opportunity of revisiting the site of the ghost for three further weeks.

'On the 27th day of July 1665, I went to the haunted field by myself, and walked the breadth of it without any encounter; I returned, and took the other walk, and then the spectrum appeared to me, much about the same place I saw it before when the young gentleman was with me. In my thoughts this moved swifter than the time before, and about ten foot distant from me on my right hand; insomuch that I had not time to speak as I determined with myself beforehand.

'The evening of this day, the parents, the son, and myself, being in the chamber where I lay, I propounded to them our going all together to the place the next morning. The morning being come, lest we should alarm the family of servants, they went under the pretence of seeing a field of wheat, and I took my horse and fetched a compass another way, and so we met at the stile we had appointed.

'Then we all four walked leisurely into the Quartils; and had passed above half the field before the ghost made its appearance. It then came over the stile just before us, and moved with that swiftness, that by the time we had gone six or seven steps it passed by. I immediately turned my head and ran after it, with the young man by my side; we saw it pass over the stile at which we entered, but no farther. I stepped upon the hedge at one place, he at another, but could discern nothing; whereas, I dare aver, that the swiftest horse in England could not have conveyed himself out of sight in that short space of time. Two things I observed in this day's appearance.

'1. That a spaniel dog, who followed the company unregarded, did bark and run away as the spectrum passed by; whence it is easy to conclude that it was not our fear or fancy which made the apparition.

'2. That the motion of the spectrum was not gradatim, or by steps, and moving of the feet; but a kind of gliding as children upon the ice or a boat down a swift river.

'But to proceed: this ocular evidence clearly convinced but withal strangely affrighted the old gentleman and his wife, who knew this Dorothy Dingley in her lifetime, were at her burial, and now plainly saw her features in this present apparition. I encouraged them as well as I could; but after this they went no more.

'The next morning, being Thursday, I went out very early by myself, and walked for about an hour's space in meditation and prayer in the field next adjoining the Quartils. Soon after five I stepped over the stile into the disturbed field, and had not gone above thirty or forty paces before the ghost appeared at the further stile. I spoke to it with a loud voice, in some such sentences as the way of these dealings directed me, whereupon it approached but slowly, and when I came near it moved not. I spoke again, and it answered, in a voice neither very audible nor intelligible. I was not in the least terrified, and therefore persisted until it spoke again, and gave me satisfaction. But the work could not be finished at this time; wherefore the same evening, an hour after sunset, it met me again in the same place, and after a few words of each side it quietly vanished; and neither doth appear since, nor will ever more to any man's disturbance. The discourse in the morning lasted about a quarter of an hour.

'These things are true, and I know them to be so with as much certainty as eyes and ears can give me; and until I can be persuaded that my senses do deceive me about their proper object, I must and will assert that these things in this paper are true.'

The figure in the road

THERE WERE SOME INTRIGUING ITEMS IN THE *EXETER EXPRESS AND ECHO* during November 1939. A letter from an Exeter businessman was published in the edition of Friday 3 November, in which he stated the following.

'I was driving towards Starcross from Exeter at about seven in the evening when I suddenly caught sight of a woman wearing a black cape standing in the centre of the road near Powderham Church. I immediately applied my brakes, thinking it was a pedestrian asking for trouble. To my amazement, as the car drew to a halt, the figure simply vanished. I got out of the car and looked all around, but there was not the slightest sign of anybody, and nowhere where anyone could have gone.

'I got in the car again and drove on, and when I drew near the churchyard I saw the figure again. This time I saw the shrouded form slip through the churchyard gate, which was closed. I had had nothing to drink that day, and had in fact come straight from business in Exeter. So far as I know

I am not psychic, and I have never seen anything of the nature before.'

Six days later there was another letter on the subject, from the newspaper's correspondent in Crediton.

'I was told what I thought was rather an interesting story by one of my friends, who said that some months ago during the dark evenings she was motoring with a friend from Exeter to Teignmouth, and when they were going down the incline by Powderham Arch close to the church, she saw something walking across the road from the right-hand side; it walked in front of the car and disappeared into the hedge.

'At the time she first saw it she did not say anything to the driver of the car, but noticed that he had suddenly slowed down, and after they had gone a few yards further she asked him why he slowed down, to which he replied, "Didn't you see something walking across the road that looked like a lady wearing a grey cloak?"'

This same man and woman, on passing the same stretch of road two weeks later, again saw the figure on the road. There was much speculation in the local press, and other people came forward with 'sightings' – one going back to 1919 – but the episode soon faded from public memory.

Strange news from Spraiton

A PAMPHLET WAS PUBLISHED, IN MAY 1683, THAT RELATED CERTAIN EVENTS concerning what was then considered to be a 'daemon'. The details were taken from a 'gentleman' of Spraiton, in Devon, as well as from the minister in the adjacent town of Barnstaple and several other witnesses. The pamphlet was entitled *The Daemon of Spraiton in Devon*. It begins thus.

'About the month of November in the year 1682, in the parish of Spraiton, in the county of Devon, one Francis Fey (servant to Mr Philip Furze) being in a field near the dwelling house of his said master, there appeared unto him the resemblance of an aged gentleman, like his master's father, with a pole or staff in his hand, resembling that he was wont to carry when living to kill the moles withal. The spectrum approached near the young man, whom you may imagine not a little surprised at the appearance of one that he knew to be dead.'

This apparition, of the old man with the pole, was only the harbinger of more extraordinary events in succeeding days and weeks. Here is an abbreviated account.

*

'[Two or three days later], the young man was riding home to his master's house in the parish of Spraiton aforesaid, when there appeared to be upon the horse behind the young man, the resemblance of the second wife of the old gentleman spoken of before.

'This daemon threw the young man off his horse and cast him with such violence to the ground as excited great astonishment not only to a gentlewoman's servant (with him), but to divers others who were spectators of the frightful action, the ground resounding with great noise by reason of the incredible force with which he was cast upon it . . . Soon after the she-spectra shewed herself to divers in the house, viz., the aforesaid young man, Mistress Thomasin Gidley, Ann Langdon, born in that parish, and a little child which, by reason of the troublesomeness of the spirit, they were fain to remove from that house.

'One time the young man's head was thrust into a very strait place betwixt a bed's head and a wall, and forced by the strength of divers men to be removed thence, and that not without being much hurt and bruised, so that much blood appeared about it: upon this it was advised that he should be bleeded, to prevent any ill-accident that might come of the bruise; after bleeding, the ligature or binder of his arm was removed from thence and conveyed about his middle, where it was strained with such violence that the girding had almost stopp'd his breath and kill'd him, and being cut asunder it made a strange and dismal noise, so that the standers-by were affrighted by it.

'At divers other times he hath been in danger to be strangled with cravats and handkerchiefs that he hath worn about his neck, which hath been drawn so close that with the sudden violence he hath near been chok'd, and hardly escaped death.

'The specter hath shewed great offence at the perriwigs which the young man used to wear, for they were very often torn from his head after a very strange manner; one that he esteemed above the rest he put in a small box, and that box he placed in another, which he set against the wall of his chamber, placed a joint-stool with other weight atop of it, but in short time the boxes were broken in sunder and the perriwig rendered into many small parts and tatters. Another time, lying in his master's chamber with his perriwig on his head, to secure it from danger, within a little time it was torn from him, and reduced into very small fragments. At another time one of his shoestrings was observed (without the assistance of any hand) to come of its own accord out of its shoe and fling itself to the other side of the room; the other was crawling after it, but a maid espying that, with her hand drew it out, and it strangely clasp'd and curl'd about her hand like a living eel or serpent; this is testified by a lady of considerable quality, too great for exception, who was an eye-witness. The same lady shewed Mr C. one of the young man's gloves, which was torn in his pocket while she was by, which is so dexter-ously tatter'd and so artificially torn that it is conceived a cutler could not have contrived an instrument to have laid it abroad so accurately, and all this was done in the pocket in the compass of one minute. It is further observable that if the aforesaid young man, or another person who is a servant-maid in the house, do wear their own clothes, they are certainly torn in pieces on their backs, but if the clothes belong to any other, they are not injured after that manner.

'Many other strange and fantastical frieks have been done by the said daemon or spirit in the view of divers persons; a barrel of salt of considerable quantity hath been observed to march from room to room without any human assistance.

'An hand-iron hath seemed to lay itself cross athwart a pan of milk that hath been scalding over the fire, and two flitches of bacon have of their own accord descended from the chimney where they were hung, and placed themselves upon the hand-iron.

'When the specter appears in the resemblance of her own person, she seems to be habited in the same cloaths and dress which the gentlewoman of the house (her daughter-in-law) hath on at the same time. Divers times the feet and the legs of the young man aforesaid have been so entangled about his neck that he hath been loosed with great difficulty; sometimes they have been so twisted about the frames of chairs and stools that they have hardly been set at liberty. But one of the most considerable instances of the malice of the spirit against the young man happened on Easter Eve, when Mrs C., the relator, was passing by the door of the house, and it was thus —

'When the young man was returning from his labour, he was taken up by the skirt of his doublet by this female daemon, and carried a height into the air. He was soon missed by his master and some other servants that had been at labour with him, and after diligent enquiry no news could be heard of him until at length (near half an hour later) he was heard singing and whistling in a bog or quagmire, where they found him in a kind of trance or extatick fit, to which he hath sometimes become accustomed (but whether before the affliction he met with from this spirit, I am not certain). He was affected much after such sort, as at the time of those fits, so that the people did not give that attention and regard to what he said as at other times; but when he returned again to himself (which was about half an hour later) he solemnly protested to them that the daemon had carried him so high that his master's house seemed to him to be but as a hay-cock, and during all that time he was in perfect sense, and prayed to Almighty God not to suffer the devil to destroy him; and that he was suddenly set down in that quagmire.

'The workmen found one shoe on one side of his master's house, and the other on the other side, and in the morning espied his perriwig hanging on the top of a tree; by which it appears he had been carried a considerable height, and that what he told them was not a fiction.

'After this it was observed that the part of the young man's body which had been on the mud in the quagmire was somewhat benumbed and seemingly deader than the other, whereupon the following Saturday, which was the day before Low Sunday, he was carried to Crediton, alias Kirton, to be bleeded, which being done accordingly, and the company having left him for some little space, at their return they found him in one of his fits, with his forehead much bruised, and swollen to a great bigness, none being able to guess how it happened, until his recovery from that fit, when upon enquiry he gave them this account of it: that a bird had with great swiftness and force flown in at the window with a stone in its beak, which it had dashed against his forehead, which had occasioned the swelling which they saw.

'The people much wondering at the strangeness of the accident, diligently sought the stone, and under the place where he sat they found not such a stone as they expected but a weight of brass or copper which it seems the daemon had made use of on that occasion to give the poor young man that hurt in his forehead.

'The persons present were at trouble to break it to pieces, everyone taking a part, and preserving it in memory of so strange an accident. After this the spirit continued to molest the young man in a very severe and rugged manner, often handling him with great extremity, and whether it hath yet left its violences to him, or whether the young man be yet alive, I can have no certain account.'

The scream

THIS IS THE NARRATIVE OF A POLICEMAN, MR TOM LANGLEY, RECORDED some years ago and published in Roy Palmer's *The Folklore of Worcestershire* (1976). Mr Langley joined the police force of Warwickshire in 1927, and began his work as a constable in Digbeth.

'About two o'clock in the morning I was in Fazeley Street talking to the sergeant. It was a cold night and, of course, apart from the occasional noise from the railway, very quiet. Suddenly there was a terrible scream. It seemed to come from the direction of Milk Street. It was spine-chilling. It crescendoed for some seconds and then stopped suddenly. I can only liken it to the shriek I once heard when a cat was killed by a fox; this was also in the night.

'I said to the sergeant, "Somebody's been killed." I expected him to move quickly, even if it was only in the wrong direction. He stood still and said, "You will hear that again if you work this beat long enough. Put it down to an engine in the sidings. Some of the old Brums round here say it's a ghost, but we are paid to catch thieves not ghosts."

'I took the sergeant's advice, put it down to a railway engine, and forgot all about it. Two years or so later I was on the beat again and I heard it. I knew at this second experience that it was not an engine, and I decided to make quiet enquiries. I mentioned it to an uncle who had been retired from the force for several years and had been on the division in 1895. He told me he had heard it several times during his twenty-five years' service, but it was better to forget it. I still was not satisfied.

'Now it happened that in a factory in Allison Street was a night-watchman. He was a pensioner, over seventy years of age. He had joined the force in 1880, and his father had been a policeman in the district in the 1850s. I spoke about this scream to him and he told me this story.

'When Prince Rupert sacked Birmingham during the Civil War in 1643, the town was mainly around the River Rea in the Digbeth area. The inhabitants knew that the Royalists were quartered on Camp Hill and practically all of them left the area and hid in the fields of Edgbaston and Winson Heath. One man, named Moore, with his wife and five children, lived in a cottage in Milk Street, and for some reason stayed put. Three of Rupert's troopers dragged the family into Digbeth, and one of them beheaded the father, mother, and the children. The last to be murdered was a girl of thirteen. She saw all her family mercilessly slaughtered, and just before it happened to her, she screamed. It was his opinion that the girl's last terrible cry was still echoing down the arches of the years.'

The explanation seems a little too obvious, deriving from many such stories of the Civil War, but the mystery of the scream itself remains.

A fantastical young man

An extract from a letter from the Bishop of Durham to the Archbishop of Canterbury, *circa* 1564.

'Among other things that be amiss here in your great cures, ye shall understand that in Blackburn there is a fantastical (and some think a lunatic) young man, which says he has spoken with one of his neighbours that died four year since or more. Divers times he says he has seen him, and talked with him, and took with him the curate, the schoolmaster, and other neighbours, which all affirm that they see him too. These things be so common here, and none of authority that will gainsay it, but rather believe and confirm it, that everyone believes it. If I had known how to examine it with authority, I would have done it.'

The hole in the wall

HERE IS THE TEXT OF A LETTER WRITTEN TO THE EDITOR OF *THE CITY PRESS* in the spring of 1907.

'Sir,

On Sunday night, while walking home down London Wall, I passed by the old piece of wall which is railed off from the road. Suddenly I was aware of a hand and arm stretched out from the railings to bar my passage. Being scared, I jumped off the pavement, and for a moment turned my back to the railings. On looking round, I saw a man dressed in dark clothes, walking back to the wall. He was wearing no hat when he reached the wall, and seemed to walk right into it. I could hear no sound of steps, and on close investigation after he disappeared I could see no man and no hole in the wall. I went on Monday to look at the place, and I cannot throw any light on the subject. Possibly some of your readers have seen the same thing. I shall be very interested to hear if they have.

'I am, etcetera,

'A READER.'

Blue Bell Hill

BEFORE THE BUILDING OF THE A229 BETWEEN ROCHESTER AND MAIDSTONE the traffic passed up a steep road, the Old Chatham Road otherwise known as Blue Bell Hill. This is an area of ancient human settlement. In a field close to the old road is the remains of a neolithic chambered tomb that has become known as 'Kit's Coty House'; in an adjacent field are a number of scattered stones that are known as 'Little Kit's Coty House'. There is a group of standing stones in the vicinity. The road itself travels over several prehistoric burials. 'Kit's Coty House' itself was erected at some date between 4300 and 3000 BC.

But Blue Bell Hill is also of more contemporary relevance. In a local Kentish newspaper, the *Maidstone Gazette* of 10 September 1968, there was a report concerning numerous sightings of a girl standing by the side of the road at eleven o'clock in the evening; she was at the bottom of the hill, close by the Lower Bell public house. She was hitch-hiking, even at this late hour. She was not in the least a faint or ghostly figure. But then unaccountably, on all occasions, she vanished. In the *Kent Evening Post* of 27 February 1969, there was another account of disappearances along the road up the hill. Mr David Smith of Rochester, for example, had several times seen two pedestrians walking up the hill; when the car came close to them, however, they disappeared. On one occasion he saw them walking down the hill, when of a sudden the two people rushed into the path of a vehicle which passed straight through them.

Then in 1974 the local police were called to the scene on two occasions when motorists believed that they had knocked down a young woman on the road; on both occasions there was no evidence of any accident or victim. The first encounter was on Saturday 13 July 1974. Mr Goodenough was driving along the Rochester to Maidstone road, when suddenly a young girl appeared in front of his vehicle. He braked and swerved, but he was sure that he had hit her; he said that he heard the sound of the impact. He left his car and found a young girl lying in the road; she was bleeding. He described her as wearing a white blouse, white ankle socks and skirt. He carried her to the side of the road, and wrapped her in a tartan rug taken from the car. Unable to flag down any passing cars, he left the girl and drove immediately to Rochester police station. He was noted as arriving at 12.15 a.m. that morning. He and the police went immediately to the scene; there was no girl, and no signs of blood. Tracker dogs were introduced the following morning, but there was no scent. There were no marks or indentations upon the car.

After this event was widely publicised there were of course innumerable local reports of phantom hitch-hikers seen at other spots on Blue Bell Hill, but none of them have been substantiated. There is, however, one interesting coincidence. An investigator, on searching through the back numbers of the *Maidstone Gazette*, discovered that three young women were killed in a car accident on Blue Bell Hill late on the evening of 19 November 1965. One of these women was to have been married on the following day.

In the autumn of 1992 three separate motorists reported that they had knocked down a young woman who had run unexpectedly into the road. A driver was quoted as saying that 'she ran in front of the car. She stopped and looked at me. There was no expression on her face. Then I hit her, and it was as if the ground moved apart and she went under the car. I thought I had killed her, because it was not as if she was see-through or anything. She was solid – as real as you are.' But of course there was no one there.

The phantom of the A38

THERE IS AN INTERESTING CASE CONCERNING AN APPARITION HAUNTING A road. The phenomenon is located on the A38 near Wellington where, over the years, there have been a number of sightings. They were widely publicised after a report in the *Western Morning News* in the summer of 1970. It described the experience of Mrs K. Swithenbank who had been driving, after dark, along this stretch of the road. As she came up to the Heatherton Grange Hotel, she rounded a bend; there to her horror she saw in the middle of the road a middle-aged man in a mackintosh. She could not see his face, but she noticed instantaneously that he was shining a torch onto the road itself. She swerved to avoid him, and then came to a halt. When she looked around there was no one on the road.

When her story was published in the newspaper, others came forward with accounts of the same figure in the mackintosh. Two drivers claimed to have seen him. One motorcyclist was reported to have broken his leg while swerving to avoid a figure staring intently down at the road.

A long-distance lorry driver, Harold Unsworth, wrote to the *Exeter Express and Echo* with his account of three encounters in the autumn of 1958. He was driving along a stretch of the A38 towards Cullompton in Devonshire, when three hundred yards ahead of him he saw the figure of a man, in a grey raincoat, standing in the middle of the road. Unsworth pulled his vehicle to a halt, naturally enough, and the man brought out a torch and flashed it in his face. It was very early in the morning, before dawn, and the man was drenched with rain; according to Unsworth, his mackintosh was saturated, and the water was running down his face. Unsworth told the man to get into his lorry, whereupon his passenger asked to be taken four miles down the road to the old bridge at Holcombe. Unsworth described his strange companion as middle-aged, with a head of unruly grey hair. Three days later, at the same time and on the same stretch of road, the lorry driver saw the man again waving his arm. Once more he gave him a lift and dropped him at the old bridge. On this occasion the passenger was smiling, and occasionally chuckling. Then, a month later, the incident reoccurred in exactly the same fashion. On each occasion the area was soaked with torrential rain. The passenger was wet through, his raincoat sodden with damp.

There were no more encounters with the figure for three months. Then towards the end of the year Mr Unsworth was following his familiar route when, on the same section of the A38, he saw the middle-aged man standing in the middle of the road and waving his torch. He felt obliged to stop for him once more. But the passenger, getting out at the old bridge, then asked Unsworth to stop for a couple of minutes so that he could 'collect some suitcases'. The driver waited for twenty minutes and then, impatient to carry on his journey, drove off. He travelled about three miles along the A38 when he saw the man again in the middle of the road. He swerved and tried to drive around the figure in the mackintosh. But the man, instead of flinching, dived in front of the heavy goods vehicle. Unsworth, thoroughly alarmed, stopped the lorry and climbed out expecting to see the body of the man somewhere beside the road. The figure was now standing further off, shaking his fist at him. Then it turned and disappeared. Mr Unsworth never saw the apparition again.

In 1973, on one dark evening, Mrs Taylor was driving along the A38 near Taunton when she saw a man standing in the middle of the road. His head was bowed, as if he were looking for something on the ground. She swerved to avoid him but, on leaving the car, she realised that there was no one near her.

In December 1991 a woman was driving along the stretch of the A38 near the village of Rumwell. Suddenly there was a man in a grey raincoat, standing in the middle of the road and flashing a torch. She was forced to swerve, and her car ended up in a ditch. She left the car to remonstrate with him, but there was nothing on the road.

The railway traveller

THE FOLLOWING ACCOUNT WAS GIVEN, IN THE 1930S, TO MAUD FFOULKES BY
Mrs Theodore Cory who was then better known as the novelist
Winifred Graham. It was later published by Maud Ffoulkes in *True
Ghost Stories* (1936).

'I was travelling from Hampton Court to Waterloo one morning, and
was lucky enough to find an empty carriage at Hampton Court. At
Thames Ditton, the next stop, quite an ordinary-looking man got
into the carriage and sat down at the far end from me. We took no
notice of each other, and in the ordinary course of events I should
have continued reading my newspaper without giving him a thought.
But I suddenly had the most dreadful feeling about him, in fact it
was so strong that I could hardly support his presence, and something seemed to say "Take in every detail of that man's appearance,
because you will have to identify him again." Naturally, after receiving
this psychic warning, I thought he might be going to attack me, and
I decided that I would get out at the next station (Surbiton), but in
the meantime I obeyed the inward order. Without appearing to
observe him, I registered in my mind his face and figure, the colour

of his clothes, and especially a little pile of four books, fastened neatly together with straps.

'So uncomfortable and nervous did I feel that I was ready to jump out of the train at the next station. But, rather to my amusement, before I had time to rise to my feet when the train drew in at Surbiton, my fellow traveller calmly took his books under his arm, stepped out and marched off. "So much for intuitions," thought I, and telling myself I was very silly, I dismissed the incident from my mind.

'Surbiton is always a busy station in the morning, and a minute later some other people got into my empty carriage, and the train proceeded to Waterloo. I closed my eyes for a little, and opened them at Vauxhall to see what station we had arrived at when, to my un-utterable horror, I saw the very same man seated in front of me. On his knee were the four books in their straps, and he sat very still, gazing quite calmly and normally at me.

'At this time, being unacquainted with the psychology of ghosts, I was frozen with terror, as I knew he had left the train at Surbiton. I got out and ran the whole length of the train, desirous of nothing except to put distance between us. Then I jumped, panting, into a compartment, terrified lest I should meet him again at Waterloo.

'Alas this ghost story has no sequel, this experience was the beginning and end of my phantom man, and I shall never be able to explain it to myself or to cease regretting my folly in doing a bolt. How often have I longed to know what would have happened had I asked the "ghost" the time, or waited to see whether he would vanish when we reached our destination.'

Only nettles

Mr Andrews of Swinbrook, in Oxfordshire, tape-recorded this event from some period in the earlier half of the last century. It was published by Katharine M. Briggs in *The Folklore of the Cotswolds* (1974).

'There were two of us saw it, and I'm not telling you just where it was because I don't want anybody to be nervous. I've never seen it since, but I was told that the same thing was seen twenty years before.

'Another fellow and I were going along the road one night, talking together like it might be you and me now, when for some reason we both suddenly stopped talking and came to a dead halt. Then we saw in front of us something blocking the road; it was jet-black and about the height of a piano. Then it changed into a column about the height and shape of a man, but seemed to be made of smoke – moving smoke, sort of zig-zag. Then it began to move; you know how a dog creeps sideways when it's frightened? It reminded me of that somehow. It came a bit towards us and a bit sideways, as if it wanted to get past. My mate pulled out his torch and flashed it on, and I took it from him and went over to where the thing was and searched, but there was nothing, only old dead stinging nettles by the roadside. "Come on," said the other chap, "there's nothing there," and we went on; but later we talked about it and we'd both seen the same thing, and he said, "I reckon it was a ghost."'

The oddity and the precision of the detail are most convincing here – 'about the height of a piano', 'how a dog creeps sideways when it is frightened', 'as if it wanted to get past'. The unexpected and individual observation does tend to bestow credibility upon what might otherwise seem to be incredible stories. One twentieth-century ghost was reported to have straight lines down both sides of its figure, as if it had been glimpsed through a gap in a wooden fence. In Hereford, in the nineteenth century, visitors were shown to an elm tree, where there was 'summat to be seen'; it was the form of a pig going up the tree backwards. In Crowborough, Sussex, there was Jarvis Brook Road; it was known, or believed, to harbour the presence of a 'spectral bag of soot' that would pursue the unwary. This has parallels with the 'jet-black' form of the first anecdote, suggesting a moving patch of darkness.

The horseman

THERE HAVE BEEN REPORTS OF VERY ANCIENT GHOSTS, SOME OF THEM dating from prehistory. In the winter of 1927 Doctor Clay was driving along the B3081 road from Cranborne to Sixpenny Handley, in Dorset, and had just passed Squirrel's Corner. This is the site of a round barrow, of which there are many in this part of the county; the landscape is also marked by a cursus some six miles in length. The area was, in other words, a place of ritual activity. As he was driving Doctor Clay suddenly caught sight of a horseman, to the north-east, who was travelling in the same direction as himself. The horse and rider came closer to the road until Doctor Clay could see them clearly. He reported that the horseman 'had long bare legs and wore a long loose cloak. The horse had a long mane and tail, but I could see no bridle or stirrups. The rider's face was turned towards me but I could not see his features. He seemed to be threatening me with an implement which he waved in his right hand above his head.' After a few moments the rider disappeared. The driver was convinced that he had seen some revenant from an earlier age of the world, riding as he had done three thousand years before. In the late 1920s, two young girls on bicycles went to the police after being terrified by a horse and rider who rode soundlessly beside them on the same stretch of road.

Witness saw no one

THERE IS AN INTERESTING ACCOUNT OF A HAUNTING AMONG EIGHTEENTH-century settlers in America; as all of the witnesses and participants were English, we may claim it fairly as an English ghost, albeit transported to foreign soil. The story was published in a pamphlet at the time, containing material taken down in a courtroom by one of the clerks of the court. These are the words, as reported by Catherine Crowe in *The Night Side of Nature* (1852).

'William Brigs said that he was forty-three years of age; that Thomas Harris died in September in the year 1790. In the March following he was riding near the place where Thomas Harris was buried, on a horse formerly belonging to Thomas Harris. After crossing a small stream, his horse began to walk on very fast. It was between the hours of eight and nine o'clock in the morning. He was alone: it was a clear day. He entered a lane adjoining to the field where Thomas Harris was buried. His horse suddenly wheeled at a portion of the fence, looked over the fence into the field where Thomas Harris was buried, and neighed very loud. Witness then saw Thomas Harris coming towards him, in the same apparel he had last seen him in his lifetime: he had on a sky-blue coat. Just before he came to the fence, he varied to the right and vanished; his horse immediately took the road. Thomas Harris came within two panels of the fence to him; he did not see his features nor speak to him. He thinks the horse knew Thomas Harris, because of his neighing, pricking up his ears, and looking over the fence.

'About the first of June following, he was ploughing in his own field, about three miles from where Thomas Harris was buried. About dusk Thomas Harris came alongside of him, and walked with him about two hundred yards. He was dressed as when first seen. He made a halt about two steps from him. John Bailey, who was ploughing along with him, came driving up, and he lost sight of the ghost. He was much alarmed: not a word was spoken. The young man Bailey did not see him; he did not tell Bailey of it. There was no motion of any particular part: he vanished. It preyed upon his mind so as to affect his health. He was with Thomas Harris when he died, but had no particular conversation with him.

'Some time after, he was lying in bed, about eleven or twelve o'clock at night, when he heard Thomas Harris groan; it was like the groan he gave a few minutes before he expired. Mrs Brigs, his wife, heard the groan. She got up and searched the house; he did not, because he knew the groan to be from Thomas Harris. Some time after, when in bed, and a great firelight in the room, he saw a shadow on the wall, and at the same time he felt a great weight upon him. Some time after, when in bed and asleep, he felt a stroke between the eyes which blackened both of them: his wife was in bed with him, and two young men were in the room. The blow awoke him, and all in the room were asleep; he is certain no one in the room struck him: the blow swelled his nose.

'About the middle of August he was alone, coming from Hickey Collins's, after dark, about one hour in the night, when Thomas

Harris appeared, dressed as he had seen him previously in a sky-blue coat. It was starlight. He extended his arms over his shoulders. Does not know how long he remained in this situation. He was much alarmed. Thomas Harris disappeared. Nothing was said. He felt no weight on his shoulders. He went back to Collins's, and got a young man to go with him. After he got home he mentioned it to the young man. He had, before this, told James Harris that he had seen his brother's ghost.

'In October, about twilight in the morning, he saw Thomas Harris about a hundred yards from his house; his head was leaned to one side; same apparel as before; his face was towards him; he walked fast and disappeared: there was nothing between them to obstruct the view; he was about fifty yards from him and alone; he had no conception why Thomas Harris appeared to him. On the same day, about eight o'clock in the morning, he was handing up blades to John Bailey who was stacking them; he saw Thomas Harrris come along the garden fence, dressed as before; he vanished, and always to the east; was within fifteen feet of him; Bailey did not see him. An hour and a half afterwards, in the same place, he again appeared, coming as before; came up to the fence; leaned on it within ten feet of the witness who called to Bailey to look there (pointing towards Thomas Harris). Bailey asked what was there. Don't you see Harris? Does not recollect what Bailey said. Witness advanced towards Harris. One or the other spoke as witness got over the fence on the same panel that Thomas Harris was leaning on. They walked off together about five hundred yards; a conversation took place as they walked; he has not the conversation in his memory. He could not understand Thomas Harris, his voice was so low.' At a later stage in these court proceedings William Brigs stated that 'he did not speak to him with the same voice as in his lifetime'.

At the end of his testimony James Bailey was called as a witness.

This is his statement. 'Bailey, who was sworn in the case, declared that as he and Brigs were stacking blades as related by Brigs, he called to witness and said, "Look there! Do you not see Thomas Harris?" Witness said, "No." Brigs got over the fence, and walked some distance — appeared by his action to be in deep conversation with some person. Witness saw no one.'

The apparitions

THERE ARE UNCOMMON EXPERIENCES THAT MAY SUGGEST FANCIFUL explanations. There was a strange story, of the nineteenth century, from Bagbury in Cornwall. A young man, a servant, was waiting in the house for his master to arrive. 'All the doors were fast locked, and every one else was in bed, when the outer door suddenly burst open, and a black man came silently in and passed through the kitchen and out at the opposite door. The youth went and fastened the doors and sat down again by the fire, but in a few minutes the same thing happened again. The doors burst open and the black man passed through the house, in at the back door and out at the front. All through that night, as often as the lad shut the doors, the same thing happened over and over again. And he never dared speak to the strange visitor, for "he took it to be the squire".'

Andrew Lang tells the story of a friend who, as a boy, was employed in a shop. 'The overseer was a dark, rather hectic-looking man, who died. Some months afterwards the boy was sent on an errand. He did his business, but, like a boy, returned by a longer and more interesting route. He stopped at a bookseller's shop to stare at the books and pictures, and while doing so he felt a kind of mental vagueness. It was just before his dinner hour, and he may have been hungry. On resuming his way, he looked up and found the dead overseer beside him. He had no sense of surprise and walked for some distance, conversing on ordinary topics with the appearance. He happened to notice such minute details as that the spectre's boots were laced in an unusual way. At a crossing, something in the street attracted his attention; he looked away from his companion and, on turning to resume their talk, saw no more of him. He then walked to the shop, where he mentioned the occurrence to a friend. He has never during a number of years had any such experience again, or suffered the preceding sensation of vagueness.'

It is sometimes said that ghosts, or phantoms, may often walk unknown among the living. There is a story, reported by Sir Walter Scott, of a woman who saw the spectre of someone she knew well. 'She said that she had seen him in public places, both in the church-yard and on the street, where he walked about among other people, and handled goods that were for sale, without attracting any notice.' The supposition here must be that the ghosts of the dead are some-times indistinguishable from 'real' people. How many do we pass in the course of a day? In Peter Moss's *Ghosts over Britain* there is an intriguing account of a figure in a wide-brimmed hat standing at a urinal in what seemed to be seventeenth-century clothes. It then disappeared. It was seen again walking down a street in Colchester where 'no one seemed to notice him, and though he did not appear to take any deliberate avoiding action he never seemed to get in anyone's way or to bump into anyone'.

For many years of the twentieth century there have been reports of a unusual figure in Swains Lane, a road that runs beside Highgate Cemetery. It is described as resembling a tall man in a hat, and his presence was attested by numerous letters in the *Hampstead and Highgate Express* in the 1970s. Here are some of the extracts from a range of correspondence: 'My fiancé spotted a most unusual form about a year ago. It just seemed to glide across the park. I am glad someone else has spotted it . . .' 'To my knowledge the ghost always takes the form of a pale figure and has been appearing for several years . . .' 'Suddenly from the corner of my eye, I saw something move which seemed to be walking towards us from the gates, and sent us running up Swains Lane as fast as we could . . .' 'My advice is to avoid Swains Lane during dark evenings, if at all possible.'

There seems to be a ghost summoned up by habitual activity or by habitual existence. From a house beside Wychwood Forest there comes an account of a man wheeling a barrow from the garden door to a little well-house across the lawn. He is seen at night, and does nothing but wheel the barrow to and fro. There are reports of ghosts sweeping up leaves, or tending fires, or simply sitting in an accustomed chair. From John Nicholson's *Folk Lore of East Yorkshire* comes the following paragraph. 'When bricklayers wish to give a reddish colour to the mortar, they use pounded tiles or bricks to mix with it. This powder is called simmon, and simmon pounding was formerly the hard labour punishment in Beverley Gaol, where there used to be a ghost having the name of Awd Simmon Beeather (Old Simmon Beater) and his appearance was dreaded by criminals more than the confinement and punishment.'

Dead parishioners and clerics have been 'seen' in their parish churches on numerous occasions. One cleaner saw a well-known figure, then dead, walking from the vestry to his usual seat; she was not at all alarmed and merely said, 'All right, Mr Braunty, I ain't going to hurt 'ee.' The *Gentleman's Magazine* of 1790 had a report of a spectre which, according to the editor, was 'the *very best ghost* which ever made its appearance in England'. The story is a short one. 'It appeared for several years but very seldom, only in the church porch at Kilncote, in Leicestershire, and was discovered by a lady now living, and *then* the rector's wife. It was not a ghost that could appear *ad libitum*; sometimes it did not appear for four years. The lady determined to approach it; and the nearer she advanced, the more confident she was that the substance or shade of a human figure was before her.'

There are also many reports of dead villagers or townspeople being 'seen' in the streets and lanes which they had frequented all of their lives. Kathleen Wiltshire, in her *Ghosts and Legends of the Wiltshire Countryside*, tells a story from the late 1940s of a neighbour seeing an old man by his gate. 'He entered the garden and walked up the path leading to his back door and disappeared as if going into his house.' The old man had recently been taken to hospital and, on the neighbour remarking to her husband that he seemed much better, she was informed that he had died that afternoon. These phenomena, if they are authentic, would suggest that the memory of human form is held in the terrain itself. These wraiths may be images on a rotating spool.

Or perhaps they are held in the atmosphere, as if in a solution. There is an anonymous pamphlet, published in January 1643, entitled *A Great Wonder in Heaven*. Two months after the battle of Edgehill, which was fought on 23 October 1642, the residents of that neighbourhood were surprised by strange sights in the sky where the battle seemed to be re-enacted. 'Between twelve and one of the clock in the morning was heard by some shepherds, and other countrey-men, and travellers, first the sound of drums afar off, and the noyse of souldiers, as it were, giving out their last groanes at which they were much amazed . . . But then, on the sudden . . . appeared in the ayre those same incorporeall souldiers that made those clamours, and immediately with Ensignes display'd, Drummes beating, Musquets going off, Cannons discharged, horses neyghing (which also to these men were visible), the alarum or entrance to this game of death was struck up . . . Till two or three in the morning, in equal scale continued this dreadful fight . . . so amazing and terrifying the poore men that they could not give credit to their eares and eyes; run away they durst not, for feare of being made a prey to these infernall souldiers, and so they, with much feare and affright, stayed to behold the outcome of the business.'

Come up here

THERE IS A STRANGE VIGNETTE, COMING FROM THE EARLIER YEARS OF THE last century, by a gentleman from Wiltshire. Mr T. W. Tilley explains that he was in the habit of cycling on three evenings a week to Melksham, a village in the county; on his return journey one night, at about 10.30, he had reached the turning to Poulshot, when someone started to whistle to him from the top of the bridge. The rest of the story is in his own words, as related in Kathleen Wiltshire's *Ghosts and Legends of the Wiltshire Countryside* (1973).

'As I got nearer, there were shouts of "Come up here, come up here"; but I did not stop. Two mornings later the body of a man, a Mr Moss (of Rowde, I think) was found on the grass verge directly beneath the high wall at the side of the bridge. If I remember rightly, the inquest brought in an open verdict. My mother always swore that would have been my fate had I gone up there.'

The call of 'come up here' is strangely arresting. It suggests both invitation, with the promise of some interesting experience, and peremptory command. It is reminiscent of the words of Jenny Wren, the dolls' dressmaker in *Our Mutual Friend*. 'Come up and be dead! Come up and be dead!'

The lady in white

There was an interesting letter in the *Hull Advertiser* of 13 August 1818, concerning an apparition in Skipsea Lane of that neighbourhood.

'Sir, about six months ago, a small party, including myself, having met at the house of a lady in Holderness, our conversation, in its range, happened to rest on the subject of supernatural appearances. The good lady of the house expressed her disbelief in the reality of such appearances, which led a gentleman of known veracity to relate what he himself had seen. "About ten years ago," he said, "as I was travelling on horseback, one afternoon in the month of March, on the road from Hornsea to Bridlington, just as I was ascending the brow of a hill on the south of Skipsea, I observed a woman, apparently young, dressed in white, walking a little before me, on my left hand, between the hedge and the road. Supposing that she had been visiting at a house on the top of the hill close by, I turned to see if there were any persons in attendance at the door, but it was shut, and none to be seen. My curiosity, being now greater than before, to know who this genteel woman was, I followed her at the distance of twenty or thirty yards down the hill, one hundred or one hundred and fifty yards long, and expected when I got to the bottom, where there was a small brook, that I should meet her in attempting to gain the carriage bridge, forming the road; but to my great astonishment, when she approached the brook, she vanished from my sight at the very time my eyes were fixed upon her. As soon as I got home I related the strange affair to my family; and as it was light, and I had not been previously thinking of apparitions, nor was I ever in the habit of speculating on such subjects, I am firmly persuaded that what I saw was one, although I never heard that there was anything ever seen there before or since."

'The lady of the house, who had listened with particular attention to this recital, said, at the conclusion of it, that what she had just heard had made a greater impression on her mind than anything she had ever heard before; for, continued she, about five years ago I had a servant, who was a young man of good character, of a bold active disposition, and who professed a disbelief in supernatural appearances. In the month of November, about Martinmas time, he requested leave to go to Bridlington, and also to be accommodated with a horse, which was granted to him. Being desirous of making a long holiday of it, he rose early in the morning and set off two hours before daybreak; but, to my great surprise, returned home in the early afternoon before it was dark. On being questioned if anything was the matter with him, he replied that he had been so much alarmed that he was resolved never to travel in the dark if he could avoid it. "For," said he, "as I was cantering along Skipsea Lane, in the morning, bending forwards with my face downward, the horse suddenly bolted from the road to such a distance that I was very nearly dismounted. On recovering, and looking about to see what had affrighted the horse, I saw a fine lady, dressed in white, with something like a black veil on her face, standing close by. How I got to Skipsea I cannot tell, but I was so frightened that I dared not go further, but walked up and down the town until it was light, when I found some person going the same road, whom I accompanied to Bridlington."'

The letter to the *Hull Advertiser* ends with the usual salutation, and makes no attempt to explain or interpret the appearances of the figure on the road.

The walking party

THIS IS A REPORT, DATED IN FEBRUARY 1907, FROM A POLICE CONSTABLE —
known as 265 T — on duty at Hampton Court Palace.

'I went on duty at the east front of the palace at ten o'clock, and had
to remain there until six o'clock next morning. I was quite alone,
and standing close to the main gates, looking towards the Home Park,
when suddenly I became conscious of a group of figures moving
towards me along what is known as the Ditton Walk. It is a most
unusual thing to see anyone in the gardens at that time of night, but
I thought it probable that some of the residents in the palace had
been to a party at Ditton and were returning on foot. The party
consisted of two gentlemen in evening dress, and seven or nine ladies.
There were no sounds except what resembled the rustling of dresses.

'When they reached a point about a dozen yards from me I turned
around and opened the gates to let them in. The party, however,
altered their course, and headed in the direction of the Flower Pot
Gates, to the north of the gardens. At the same time there was a
sudden movement among the group; they fell into a processional
order, two deep, with the gentlemen at their head. Then, to my utter

amazement, the whole crowd of them vanished; melted, as it seemed to me, into the air. All this happened within nine yards of where I was standing, in the centre of the broad gravel walk in front of the palace. I rushed to the spot, looked up and down, but could see nothing or hear nothing to explain the mystery.'

Clerical souls

Palms outwards

WILLIAM WORDSWORTH GAVE AN ACCOUNT TO WILLIAM HOWITT, AUTHOR of *History of the Supernatural*, in which he related a visit by an undergraduate to his nephew, Christopher Wordsworth, who was a Fellow and tutor of Trinity College, Oxford. According to the poet's account a young man, having just come to enter himself as a student at Trinity, brought with him a letter of introduction to Dr Wordsworth. On presenting the letter the young man asked Wordsworth if he could recommend comfortable lodgings in the vicinity. Dr Wordsworth did then mention some that were vacant at the time, and the young man took them.

A few days after this Wordsworth, seeing the young student, asked him how he liked his new quarters. He replied that the rooms themselves were very comfortable, but that he should be obliged to give them up. Upon being asked his reasons, the young undergraduate replied that Dr Wordsworth might think him fanciful, but that the rooms were haunted, and that he had been woken up each night by the apparition of a child, which wandered about the rooms moaning, and, strange to say, with the palms of his hands turned outwards; that he had searched his rooms, and on each occasion had found them securely locked, and that he was convinced that nothing but an apparition could have traversed them.

Dr Wordsworth said he would now be candid with him, and confess that these rooms had been repeatedly abandoned by students on the plea that they were haunted, but that, having perfect reliance on his judgement and veracity, from what he had heard of him, he wanted to see whether he would confirm the story – having no intimation of it in advance.

William Howitt then goes on to observe, 'whether the young man thanked Dr Wordsworth for his recommendation of such lodgings, does not appear'.

The boy in the schoolroom

THIS NARRATIVE, SET IN THE DORSET TOWN OF BEAMINSTER, WAS published in *The Gentleman's Magazine* (1774).

'The school of Beaminster is held in the gallery of the parish church to which there is a distinct entrance from the churchyard. Every Saturday the key of it is delivered to the clerk of the parish by one or other of the schoolboys. On Saturday June 27, 1728, the master had dismissed his lads as usual. Twelve of them loitered about in the churchyard to play at ball. It was just about noon. After a short space four of the lads returned into the school to search for old pens, and were startled by hearing in the church a noise which they described as that produced by striking a brass pan. They immediately ran to their playfellows in the churchyard and told them of it. They came to the conclusion that someone was hiding in order to frighten them, and they all went back in the school together to discover who it was, but could not find anyone. As they were returning to their sport, on the stairs that lead into the churchyard, they heard in the school a second noise. Terrified at that, they ran round the church, and when at the belfry, or west door, they heard what seemed to them the sound of someone preaching, which was succeeded by another sound as of a congregation singing psalms. Both of these noises lasted but a short time.

'With the thoughtlessness of youth the lads soon resumed their sport, and after a short time one of them went into his school for his book, when he saw a coffin lying on one of the benches, only about six feet away. Surprised at this, he ran off and told his playfellows what he had seen, on which they all thronged to the school-door, whence *five* of the twelve saw the apparition of John Daniel, who had been dead more than seven weeks, sitting at some distance from the coffin, further in the school. All of them saw the coffin, and it was conjectured why all did not see the apparition was because the door was so narrow they could not all approach it together. The first who knew it to be the apparition of their deceased school-fellow was Daniel's half-brother; and he, on seeing it, cried out "There sits our John, with such a coat on as I have!" (in the lifetime of the deceased boy the half-brothers were usually clothed alike) "with a pen in his hand and a book before him, and a coffin by him. I'll throw a stone at him." The other boys tried to stop him, but he threw the stone – as he did so, saying "Take it". Upon which the apparition immediately disappeared.

'The immense excitement this created in the place may be imagined. The lads, whose ages ranged from nine to twelve, were all magisterially examined by Colonel Broadrepp, and all agreed in their relation of the circumstance, even to the hinges of the coffin; whilst their description of the coffin tallied exactly with that the deceased had been buried in. One of the lads who saw the apparition was quite twelve years of age; he entered the school after the deceased had left it (on account of illness about a fortnight before his death), and had never seen Daniel in his lifetime. This lad, on examination, gave an exact description of the person of the deceased, and took especial notice of one thing about the apparition which the other boys had not observed, and that was, it had a white cloth or rag bound around one of its hands. The woman who laid out the corpse of John Daniel for interment deposed on oath that she took such a white cloth from his hand, it having been put on the boy's hand (he being lame of it) about four days or so before his death. Daniel's body had been found in an obscure place in a field, at about a furlong distant from his mother's house, and had been buried without an inquest in consequence of his mother alleging that the lad had been subject to fits.

'After the appearance of the apparition the body was disinterred, a coroner's inquest was held, and a verdict returned to the effect that the body had been "strangled". This verdict appears to have been mainly arrived at in consequence of the depositions of two women of good repute that two days after the corpse was found they saw it and discovered a "black list" around its neck; and likewise of the joiner who put the body in the coffin, and who had the opportunity of observing it, as the shroud was not put on in the usual way, but was in two pieces, one laid under and the other over the body. A surgeon who gave evidence could not, or would not, positively affirm to the jury that there was any dislocation of the neck. So far as can be learnt, no steps were taken to bring anyone to justice on account of the suggested death by violence of the lad.'

The visitor in the library

In the *Athenaeum* of January 1880, the antiquary Dr Augustine Jessop explains the events during his visit to the residence of Lord Orford in Norfolk in the previous October; he had travelled there to take notes from some rare books in Lord Orford's library. After dinner he was taken to the library, where he set to work with some six small volumes which he had taken from the shelves and had placed on the right-hand side of the desk at which he sat. He had finished with five of these volumes, and was then proceeding with the final one. The rest of the narrative can be told in his own words.

'I had been engaged upon it for about half an hour, and was just beginning to think that my work was drawing to a close, when, as I was actually writing, I saw a large white hand within a foot of my elbow. Turning my head, there sat a figure of a somewhat large man, with his back to the fire, bending slightly over the table, and apparently examining the pile of books that I had been at work upon. The man's face was turned away from me, but I saw his closely cut reddish-brown hair, his ear and shaved cheek, the eyebrow, the corner of the right eye, the side of the forehead, and the large high cheek-bone.

He was dressed in what I can only describe as a kind of ecclesiastical habit of thick-corded silk, or some such material, close up to the throat, and a narrow rim or edging, of about an inch broad, of satin or velvet, serving as a stand-up collar, and fitting close to the chin. The right hand, which had first attracted my attention, was clasping, without any great pressure, the left hand; both hands were in perfect repose, and the large blue veins of the right hand were conspicuous. I remember thinking that the hand was like the hand of Velazquez's magnificent *Dead Knight* in the National Gallery.

'I looked at my visitor for some seconds, and was perfectly sure that he was not a reality. A thousand thoughts came crowding upon me, but not the least feeling of alarm, or even uneasiness; curiosity and a strong interest were uppermost. For an instant I felt eager to make a sketch of my friend, and I looked at a tray on my right for a pencil; then I thought, "Upstairs I have a sketch-book — shall I fetch it?" There he sat, and I was fascinated; afraid not of his staying, but *lest he should go*.

'Stopping in my writing, I lifted my left hand from the paper, stretched it out to the pile of books, and moved the top one. I cannot explain why I did this — my arm passed in front of the figure, and it vanished. I was simply disappointed and nothing more. I went on with my writing as if nothing had happened, perhaps for another five minutes, and had actually got the last few words of what I had determined to extract, when the figure appeared again, exactly in the same place and attitude as before. I saw the hands close to my own; I turned my head again to examine him more closely, and I was framing a sentence to address him when I discovered that I dare not speak. I was afraid of the sound of my own voice. There he sat, and there sat I. I turned my head again to my work, and finished writing the two or three words I still had to write. The paper and my notes are at this moment before me, and exhibit not the slightest tremor or nervousness. I could point out the words I was writing when the phantom came, and when he disappeared. Having finished my task, I shut the book and threw it on the table; it made a slight noise as it fell – the figure vanished.

'Throwing myself back in my chair, I sat for some seconds looking into the fire with a curious mixture of feeling, and I remember wondering whether my friend would come again, and if he did whether he would hide the fire from me. By this time I had lost all sense of uneasiness. I blew out the four candles and marched off to bed, where I slept the sleep of the just or the guilty – I know not which – but I slept very soundly.

'I decline to proffer any explanation, theory or inference about this spectral illusion.'

The church at Langenhoe

THE VICAR OF ST MARY AT LANGENHOE, A VILLAGE SOUTH OF COLCHESTER, kept a diary at the time of his appointment to the living in the autumn of 1937. The Reverend Ernest Merryweather was not previously interested in unusual phenomena, but the events beside and within the church were so striking that he kept a contemporaneous record of them in the diary. The first entry is the following.

'I visited the church on 20 September 1937. It was a quiet autumn day. I was standing alone in the church, and the big west door was wide open. Suddenly it crashed to with such force that the whole building seemed to shake. Doors don't usually slam as if an express train had hit them, when there is no palpable reason. This aroused my curiosity as to the cause.'

This is a subsequent entry.

'On 5 November, after the 11 o'clock service, I was about to leave the vestry and placed my robes in my valise. Having forgotten to put something else inside, I tried to open the catches for some time, then gave it up as hopeless; they were fixed tight. When I reached the bottom of the church lane, I tried again. The influence had gone, and the catches worked normally.'

All was quiet for eight years. Then in 1945 the vicar reported another incident out of the ordinary. His housekeeper and her young daughter, together with the Reverend Merryweather, were busy decorating the interior of the church in preparation for Easter. The housekeeper had just placed some flowers in a vase, and had put it on a pew while she was dusting; the vicar and the young girl were not near her. Moments later she turned around, to discover that the flowers had been taken out of the vase and placed neatly on the pew itself.

Three years passed. In the summer of 1948 the vicar, and several members of his congregation, heard noises coming from behind the closed door of the vestry as if clods of earth were being thrown around; it was a dull, thudding sound. On investigation, there was no obvious explanation for the noises that were heard on ten separate occasions throughout that year.

In November 1948, he had gone into the churchyard to fetch some coal. He had an iron rod to loosen the coal, and thrust it into the pile. On an impulse he put his biretta onto the rod. Much to his surprise, the biretta began to revolve slowly. In this same period there was an outbreak of violence in the neighbourhood, with the boys of a nearby village attacking local people. The Reverend Merryweather remembered that his son had bought him a dagger as a souvenir of a holiday in Cyprus; so he wore it in his belt as a precaution. He was standing, in the same month, before the altar when he felt the dagger being taken from his belt. It fell to the ground. Then he heard a female voice, somewhere behind him. 'You are a cruel man,' she said. There was no one visible in the church. In the following month there were inexplicable noises within the church. One was like that of a rifle shot; there was a sound of coughing; the credence bell rang of its own accord on several occasions.

On 21 August 1949, the Reverend Merryweather was distributing holy communion to his parishioners when he suddenly looked up. He saw the figure of a woman standing against the north wall of the church. He estimated her age in the mid-thirties; he noticed a scarf, or some other kind of headdress, that fell across her shoulders. She walked, with a slight but noticeable stoop, across the chancel and towards a corner of the south-west wall. At this point she vanished. The Reverend Merryweather affirmed that she seemed to him to be as real as any living person. It was later discovered that at the exact place she disappeared there had once been a doorway into the internal tower wall. There was now a statue of St George upon a table, in front of what had once been the door. The Reverend Merryweather was not aware of the location of the old doorway at the time of the incident.

In January 1950, while the reverend was examining the south doorway, he twice heard the sound of a sharp 'Ow!' from a female. There was no one else in the church at the time.

In the summer of that year a local bricklayer, William Ware, was asked to repair some tiles on the roof of the church. He had been given the key to the vestry door but, despite repeated attempts, the door would not open. It was to all intents and purposes sealed. Mr Ware went to a cottage close by, to ask for assistance, but when he returned with the cottager the door opened with ease. So he prepared for his work on the roof. He brought in his ladder and placed it so that he could ascend to the upper part of the church. He was surprised, when he reached the top of the ladder, by the sound of the church bell ringing – even though he knew that there was no one else in the church.

On the morning of 14 September, the unmistakable scent of spring violets filled the church.

On the evening of 28 September the Reverend Merryweather was working in the vestry when he heard the voice of a woman apparently singing plainchant. The music was then succeeded by the sound of a man's footsteps, heavy ones, proceeding along the nave. By the time the reverend had entered the body of the church, the noises had stopped.

One week later the Reverend Merryweather was surprised to find two labourers crouched down looking through the keyhole of the west door. When he walked over to them they asked him to put his ear up to the door and listen. He could plainly hear the sound of plainchant, apparently in French, being sung in the empty church. One of the workmen declared that it was odd that the singer should have locked the door, whereupon the vicar informed him that the church was empty. Both men professed disbelief, so the Reverend Merryweather took one of the men with him and entered the church through the smaller priest's door; then he opened the west door, and the three men searched the interior thoroughly. No one was found. The two men had been working at the manor, nearby, and had heard the singing.

Over the next few weeks the door of the cupboard in the vestry was commonly found open, even though it had been securely locked the night before. On one occasion the Reverend Merryweather found that his stole had been wrapped around his alb.

On Christmas Eve, alone in the church, the vicar saw a form slowly walking in front of him along the nave; it disappeared into the pulpit. The Reverend Merryweather described it as a man in modern dress, wearing what might have been a tweed suit.

Candles disappeared, or went out unexpectedly. On Saturday 23 June 1951 there was another incident. At the moment when the saint was named, the vicar and congregation were surprised by a loud noise; at the same moment, a candle on the credence table sputtered, hissed and went out. At the end of his sermon on 24 June the congregation also witnessed a strange phenomenon; a lamp hanging above a side altar exploded, bursting into flame. Throughout this period there were also sudden noises, one of them like a 'pop' when a cork is taken from a wine bottle. There were no obvious explanations for these sounds.

On Sunday 8 July the Reverend Merryweather once more glimpsed the figure of the woman whom he had seen on the previous occasion; she was standing in the aisle, wearing the same scarf, before disappearing through the stone image of St George that blocked the forgotten door.

On 8 June 1952 the vicar was aware of a 'vile smell', like that of putrefaction, at the west end of the church.

On 5 August 1952, the Reverend Merryweather was in the vestry when he heard voices within the church. They came from the area of the chancel, and seemed to be engaged in an animated if whispered conversation. The vicar could make out the sound of a male voice, but the words were all indistinct. The murmured conversation was then followed by a long, distressed sigh. The vicar immediately entered the church, but there was no one visible.

On Sunday 12 October 1952, he was conducting a service. He was singing Psalm 119 and had reached the passage 'rivers of waters run down mine eyes, because they keep not thy law' when he was aware of a stranger watching him from the vicinity of the lectern. She had an oval face, blue eyes, and was wearing a cream dress. According to the vicar she had a 'strange sad look' before melting away.

On 2 November there was a sudden terrible noise from the tower end of the church. The Reverend Merryweather was convinced that the tower was falling but, on hasty inspection, there was nothing whatever the matter with the fabric of the building.

More strange incidents occurred throughout the 1950s; doors rattled as if someone were attempting to get in; there were sounds of footsteps; lamps exploded. These incidents were widely reported in the local press, and they prompted stories and memories of stories concerning the old church – many of them going back to the early years of the twentieth century. Of course it soon became known as 'the most haunted church in England'. The Reverend Merryweather retired in 1959, and the church fell out of use. It was left to decay until it was finally demolished in 1962.

The nun of Barking

IN THE LATE SEVENTH CENTURY THERE WAS A NOVICE-MISTRESS AT Barking Abbey, Tortgith, who was blessed with the faculty of second sight. She was leaving her cell just before dawn, to be present at Matins, when she saw a body draped in a sheet hovering above the ground. Slowly it ascended into the heavens, and it seemed to Tortgith that it was being lifted by cords brighter than the brightest gold. She knew then that one of the holy ones of the abbey was about to die. A few days later the mother of the nuns, Ethelberga, left this life.

The time came, however, when Tortgith would speak to her again. She was struck with paralysis, to such an extent that her limbs were helpless. She lay immobile, and had lost the use of her tongue. She could no longer open her eyes. In this condition she remained, suffering in silence, for three days and three nights. Then, on the fourth day, her eyes opened. Much to the astonishment of the nuns who ministered to her, she began to speak. 'Your coming is very acceptable to me,' she said. 'You are most welcome here.' She seemed to be addressing the empty space at the bottom of her narrow bed. She was silent for a while, and seemed to be listening intently to a voice that the others could not hear. Then Tortgith shook her head.

'I am not at all pleased with this,' she said. There was another pause, while she listened to what was being said. 'If it cannot be today,' she replied, 'then I request that there will not be a long delay.' Again she listened. 'Well, if it has been decided, and the decision cannot be revoked, then I ask you to make sure that it happens by tomorrow night.'

The nuns then asked her to explain her words. 'I have been talking,' she told them, 'to my dear mother Ethelberga. She stood here before me. Did you not see her?' The nuns then understood that Ethelberga had come to her in order to acquaint her with the time of her death. On the following night, Tortgith died.

The ghosts in the window

A CURIOUS CORRESPONDENCE WAS STARTED IN THE SPRING OF 1869 between a clergyman known only as 'A.B.' and Sabine Baring-Gould, a famous antiquarian of the period. They had been schoolboys together, and the clergyman now wished to acquaint Baring-Gould with the strange phenomena that clustered around a window in the church of the Trinity at Micklegate, York. 'I confess,' he wrote, 'the impression left on my nerves was not pleasant, and I do not think I should like to risk the effect of a repetition of it.' The clergyman then enclosed an account that he had written in 1866. It is as follows.

'While staying in York at this time last year, or perhaps a little earlier, I first heard of the apparitions of ghosts supposed to be seen in Trinity Church, Micklegate. I felt curious to see a ghost, I confess, without the usual concomitants of a dark night and a lone house. Accordingly I went to the church for morning service on a blazing hot Sunday morning in August last, with a girl of about thirteen years old and her little brother.

'The east window of the church, I must explain, is of stained glass, rather tawdry, and of no particular design, except that the colouring is much richer at the centre than at the sides, and that at the extreme edge there is one pane of unstained glass which runs all round the window.

'The peculiarity of the apparition is that it is seen on the window itself. The form seen — I am told invariably — is that of a figure dressed in white walking across the window, and gives the idea of someone passing in the churchyard in a surplice. I say a figure, for the number is generally limited to one, and I was told that only on Trinity Sunday did more than one appear, and that then there were three.

'But I can vouch for the larger number appearing on other occasions, as on the day I was there, which was one of the Sundays after Trinity, there were rarely fewer than three visible.

'The figures began to move across the window long before the commencement of the service, when in fact there was no one present but ourselves. They did so again before the service began, as well as during the "Venite" and subsequently as many as twenty or thirty times, I should suppose, till the conclusion of the sermon.

'Of the three figures two were evidently those of women, and the third was a little child. The two women were very distinct in appearance. One was tall and very graceful; and the other middle-sized; we called the second one the nursemaid, from her evident care of the child during the absence of the mother, which relationship we attributed to the tall one, from the passionate affection she exhibited towards the child, her caressing it, and the wringing of her hands over it.

'I may add that each figure is perfectly distinct from the others, and after they had been seen once or twice are at once recognisable.

'The order of proceedings, with slight variation, was this: the mother came alone from the north side of the window, and having gone about halfway across, stopped, turned around, and waved her arms towards the quarter whence she had come. This signal was answered by the entry of the nurse with the child. Both figures then bent over the child, and seemed to bemoan its fate; but the taller one was always the most endearing in her gestures. The mother then moved towards the other side of the window, taking the child with her, leaving the nurse in the centre of the window, from which she gradually retired to the north corner, whence she had come, waving her hand, as though making signs of farewell, as she retreated.

'After some little time she again appeared, bending forward, and evidently anticipating the return of the other two, who never failed to reappear from the south side of the window where they had disappeared.

'The same gestures of distress and despair were repeated, and then all three retired together to the north side of the window.

'Usually they appeared during the musical portions of the service, and especially during one long eight-line hymn, when – for the only occasion without the child – the two women rushed on (in stage phrase) and remained during the whole hymn, making the most frantic gestures of despair. Indeed the louder the music in that hymn, the more carried away with their grief did they seem to be.

'Nothing could be more emphatic than the individuality of the several figures; the manner of each had its own peculiarity. I do not doubt that if the stained glass were removed, a much plainer view would be obtained. I think so, because the nearer the centre of the window, where the stained glass was thickest, there the less distinct were the forms. It was like catching glimpses of them through leaves. But nearer the edge of the window, where the colours were less bright, they were perfectly distinct; and still more so on the pane of unstained glass at the edge. There they seemed most clear, and gave one the impression of being real persons, not shadows.

'Indeed by far the most remarkable and perplexing incident in the whole spectacle was this, that on one occasion, when the mother and child had taken their departure, the medium figure – the nurse – waved her hands, and after walking slowly to the very edge of the window, turned round whilst on the pane of unstained glass and waved her arm towards the other two with what one would call a stage gesture, and then I most distinctly saw, and emphatically declare I did see, the arm bare nearly to the shoulder, with beautiful folds of drapery hanging from it like a picture on a Greek vase. Nothing could be plainer than the drag of the robes on the ground after the figures as they retired at the edge of the window, where the clear glass was, previous to going out. The impression produced was that one saw real persons in the churchyard, for though the figures were seen on the window, yet they gave one the impression of walking past the window outside, and not moving upon the glass.

'No one in the church seemed to be in the smallest degree attracted or discomposed by all this, or, indeed, to observe it.

'I talked a great deal on the subject with Miss C—, daughter of the late Dr C— of York, and she told me that Mr W—, the incumbent of Trinity Church, would give anything to get rid of it, or discover the imposture, if imposture there be. She told me that he and his family had watched day and night without being able to find any clue to the mystery. Their house is in the churchyard and opposite the east window, and therefore very favourably placed for such an investigation. I am not inclined to think that the trees outside the church at the east end can originate the appearance by any optical illusion produced by waving branches. I could see their leaves rustling in the air, and their movement was evidently unconnected with the appearance and movement of the figures.'

So ended the letter from 'A.B.' to Sabine Baring-Gould. Baring-Gould became interested in the curious case, and began making enquiries in the immediate neighbourhood of Micklegate itself.

He discovered that several people had indeed seen the shapes upon the glass. One spoke of a female figure with a slightly 'skipping' step. One correspondent reported that 'for some time I could hardly get up from the seat or find my place at the beginning of the chant'. Baring-Gould established that the sill of the east window was approximately five feet from ground level, and at the side of it was an ancient gravestone. The belief that the trees beside the east window were somehow responsible for the optical 'illusion' was soon dashed; the trees were cut down, but the figures appeared still. Sabine Baring-Gould was informed that the apparition, if such it was, was described in a seventeenth-century history of York; so it is of some antiquity. One correspondent wrote to him in the spring of 1874, explaining that 'as I have no faith in ghosts I have been most wishful to have the matter cleared up. At present I cannot account for the appearance in any way.' This correspondent, 'L.S.', then went on to describe a visit to the church on a dull and rainy day when he saw in the window 'a graceful figure of a girl of eighteen or twenty years'; the girl seemed to be walking a few feet beyond the window. There were of course several stories concocted around these three figures. Some said that they issued from the grave beside the east window. Others said that they were victims of the plague, and were buried outside the city wall. It may or may not be relevant that the figures seemed to appear with the sound of the organ and of voices raised in song.

The case was thoroughly investigated by the *Newcastle Daily Chronicle* in 1876, where it was revealed that the church had been 'haunted' for two or three hundred years by the same figure or figures. Optical tests on the possible patterns of light and reflection had come to no result. It was remarked that 'the ghost has been seen from the inside while outside nothing was visible'. There were theories that a swing pane of glass in a nearby cottage might have been responsible, or that the figures were the shadows of real people walking in the vicarage garden behind a wall, but these proved to be false.

The interior of the church was much altered in the late nineteenth century, and even the east window has now gone, to be replaced by one in a different position. But no satisfactory explanation has ever been given for the strange phenomena reported here. There is a short notice about the figures still to be found on the church information board attached to the gate. There have been no recent sightings.

Borley Rectory

For many years Borley Rectory had the reputation of being 'the most haunted house in England'. It has been the subject of several books and of innumerable articles, none of which can be said to be conclusive. The general conclusion seems to be that the evidence is contrary and unreliable, and that some of the supposed events were the product of fraud or chicanery. It provides, at least, an interesting story.

The rectory stood in the village of Borley, two and a half miles from Sudbury in the county of Suffolk. It lies on the north bank of the River Stour. The church itself was erected in the late twelfth century, with some evidence of Saxon material, and rebuilt at the beginning of the sixteenth century. The rector of this church, Henry D. E. Bull, built the famous or infamous rectory in 1863 on the site of a previous rectory belonging to the Herringham family. Bull built another wing to the new house in 1875, so that the entire property contained some thirty rooms. Henry Bull's son, Harry, had also entered the Church and had become curate to his father; on the death of Henry Bull in 1892, Harry succeeded him as rector, in which post he remained until his own death in 1927.

During the period of the Bulls there were peculiar incidents and sightings confirming the overwhelming feeling that this was an 'odd' house. The three daughters of Henry Bull – Ethel, Frieda and Mabel – were returning from a garden party one June afternoon; when they entered the garden of the house, all three of them saw the figure of a nun walking slowly on the other side of the lawn. This nun had been often seen at dusk or at twilight, but not before on a bright afternoon. The family had already been intrigued by the phenomenon. The spectre of a nun was supposed to walk along a path that skirted the lawn of the property, soon becoming known as Nun's Walk, and in fact Henry Bull constructed a summer-house on the other side of the lawn so that visitors could wait and watch for the dark shape. One of the windows in the dining room, overlooking the garden, was bricked up so that the Bull family would not be disturbed at their meals.

During the incumbency of Harry Bull himself there were frequent episodes of intense activity. There were footsteps, tappings and spectral appearances. One of his sisters was sometimes woken up at night by a slap on the face. Harry Bull was also aware of strange sounds within the church itself, in particular, odd knockings that seemed to approach the church porch, enter the building and then work their way around its walls. On one occasion a group of children in a catechism class distinctly heard footsteps coming along the church path and then a key turning in the lock of the church door. When their teacher arrived a few moments later, the door was locked. There have been other reports of footsteps in the porch, of the latch being lifted, and of the door being locked.

On the death of Harry Bull his family, who seemed to have some proprietorial interest in the matter, now searched for a new rector who might live in the large and somewhat ugly house. Many prospective candidates came and, when they saw the house, went. No one seemed to feel comfortable in the rectory itself. Then in the autumn of 1928, after sixteen months of fruitless search, the Bull family found a rector. The Reverend G. Eric Smith, together with his wife, took up residence in the rectory. They left nine months later. The *Daily Mirror* of 10 June 1929 reported that the Smiths 'had been puzzled and startled by a number of peculiar happenings'.

On numerous occasions they heard the sound of 'slow dragging footsteps' in an unoccupied room. Doors were unaccountably locked from the inside. All the serving bells in the house would ring unexpectedly, and for no reason; lights were seen burning in empty and unlocked rooms. Heavy wooden shutters were pulled sharply together. The mirror on Mrs Smith's dressing table would begin tapping whenever she came close to it. These alarming incidents became a daily, and nightly, occurrence. On one occasion the Reverend Smith was crossing the landing when he heard what he described as 'whisperings' above his head, which were quickly followed by 'mutterings'. He declared that it was a woman's voice; he could not make out any of the words except for a clearly enunciated, 'Don't, Carlos.' No one of that name can be associated with the rectory.

The Smiths endured Borley Rectory for nine months, but the staff of the house were not so patient. One maid-servant from London left after only two days of employment, asserting that she had seen the spectre of a nun; her successor, knowing nothing of the previous maid's experience, swore that she had seen a nun leaning over a gate near the house.

Alerted by the articles in the *Daily Mirror* Mrs Myford, who had been a maid in the house forty-three years before, described the existence of such phenomena in that earlier period. 'When I had been there a fortnight,' she wrote, 'something awakened me in the dead of night. Someone was walking down the passage towards the door of my room, and the sound they made suggested they were wearing slippers.' On subsequent enquiry she discovered that no one had been in her part of the house. Like the maids forty-three years later, she left her employment. For six months after the departure of the Smiths, the house remained empty.

Then in October a cousin of the Bulls, the Reverend L. A. Foyster, happily arrived on the scene after a long period of missionary work in India. He became rector, and entered the rectory with his wife, Marianne, and an adopted daughter named Adelaide. He also kept a diary, and on the first day of their residence he made the following notes.

'A voice calling Marianne's name; footsteps heard by self, Marianne and Adelaide and man working in the house. "Harry Bull" seen at different times by Marianne . . .' It was not the most welcome introduction to Borley Rectory. The most puzzling aspects of their experience were writings on the walls. Scrawled messages appeared, without warning, asking 'Marianne' for 'help'. The longest of them was found across an arch on the landing, 'Get light and prayers here'. Some of these appeared even as the wall was being investigated by other witnesses. The writing was extensively photographed and analysed. It was done with a graphite pencil, and seemed to experts to be 'characterless'. The jagged nature of the writing suggests that it was done with difficulty but urgently and almost impatiently; the letters begin firmly but then trail off, as if the agent had weakened or been interrupted. Their appearance has never been explained.

Mrs Foyster was walking along the upstairs landing one after-noon when she heard footsteps behind her; she turned and saw the figure of a man that promptly disappeared. She saw the same man on other occasions; he was wearing a dressing gown and was carrying a small case or large wallet. Later, on seeing photographs of previous occupants, she recognised the man as the late Harry Bull. Objects disappeared, and reappeared in other places. Most curiously of all, books appeared out of nowhere. On one afternoon the Reverend Foyster found a collection of books stacked on a kitchen rack. These books were of some age, and were of a theological nature.

At eleven o'clock one night the reverend was in the bathroom when he heard his wife cry out. According to his diary, completed at the time, she told him that 'I had been in the bedroom and had just come out on the landing when something hit me in the face and nearly stunned me for a moment. I was carrying the candle but I saw no one or anything.' There was indeed a cut under her left eye, and the blood from it was running down her face. Two of her neighbours, Sir George Whitehouse and his wife, who had also witnessed events within the house, insisted that the Foysters should take refuge with them for a time.

On their return to Borley Rectory there was another puzzling incident. The Reverend Foyster went out into the hall one evening; to his surprise he discovered that all of the pictures had been taken from the walls of the staircase and had been deposited face down on the floor of the hallway itself. Walking sticks were seen to move. A plain gold ring was found outside the door of the bathroom. It belonged to no one in the house, but its hallmark showed it to have been made in Birmingham in 1863. This was the date on which the building of the rectory was completed. The ring was gone the following day.

Borley Rectory was eventually sold to a Captain Gregson. During his occupation of the house strangers described noises (in particular, footsteps) as well as the unexplained movement of heavy objects. He was in the yard of the rectory one evening, with his black cocker spaniel, when he heard footsteps at the far end of the yard; these steps crossed a wooden trap-door, making a considerable noise. The dog stopped at once and, in Captain Gregson's own words, 'positively went mad. He shrieked and tore away, still shrieking, and we have not seen or heard of him since.' It was in the period of his occupancy that the whole house was destroyed by fire in February 1939. Captain Gregson had been sorting some books in the hall when a stack of volumes fell over, and knocked over a paraffin lamp which flooded the hall and ignited. The rectory was soon suffused in flame. It was never rebuilt, but instead left to rot and decay until it was finally demolished in 1944.

Yet the story did not end with the fiery destruction of the rectory itself. The charred remains of the house, with its few blackened timbers and walls left standing, were still an echo chamber for the sounds of footsteps and of doors slamming. The nun herself was seen again. A distinguished businessman, in the company of his two sons (both of them RAF officers), was visiting the famous ruined site. Suddenly he felt that he was being 'jumped upon' by some invisible agency that flung him into a pool of muddy water. It has been suggested, by the way, that the power or force at work was not very intelligent, and was neither altruistic nor malignant; it behaved, according to Harry Price, in *The Most Haunted House in England*, as a 'demented female'. The nun was intermittently sighted in the 1940s and 1950s. The Reverend Stanley Kipling, arriving to read the lesson at a friend's funeral, was standing by the west porch of Borley Church when he glimpsed the figure of a girl – her face veiled – walking swiftly towards some shrubs and bushes before disappearing.

There were phenomena that seemed to circulate within the church itself, after the rectory had been destroyed. One visitor, Mr John May, recorded the impressions of a visit to the church on 15 September 1947. 'The light was clear,' he wrote. 'The footsteps continued, but there was no one near. I sensed someone passing me, there was a chilliness in the air, and I felt a slight pressure. Whatever it was, I knew and felt that it was essentially evil. I also knew that I resented in some way hearing and not seeing. I then heard the sound of a key in the lock, then the creak of the door hinges as the door opened. I heard the door close. A few seconds later I heard soft notes and chords from the organ. The time was 12.18.' Mr May also stated that there was 'no tune' to the notes, and he likened them to the sounds of atonal music.

That music has been heard by others. One afternoon in October 1947, one month after the visit of John May to Borley Church, Mrs Norah Walrond was walking around the church with the new rector, the Reverend Mr Henning. 'As we were walking up the path to the south door,' she wrote, 'I stopped and said, "The organ is playing." My first thought was that there was a service in progress and that we would not therefore go in. The rector stopped and looked at me. He turned and beckoned me with a smile, so I thought that he had found it was just someone practising. To my amazement the church was empty and silent. We sat down near the organ for a moment and he said, "Have you heard the story of the organ playing before?" I assured him that I had not . . . We afterwards went up and down the path several times to see if we could hear it again but could not. The whole event was over in half a minute, and it was absolutely impossible for anyone to have escaped in that time.'

And then there were the smells associated with the church. They have been compared to the overwhelming odour of incense, but one who experienced them does not agree. Miss Susanna Dudley and some companions were walking up the church path one February afternoon when they were assailed by a rank odour. 'I can't describe the smell, really,' Miss Dudley reported, 'as I have never smelt anything like it before in my life . . . Personally the thought that passed through my mind was that it smelt as I *imagine* balm — an embalmed body would smell. I have no foundation for this, as I have never smelt an embalmed body. But at the time a sudden thought of "disgusting, like an embalmed body" struck me, so if you can imagine, too, an embalmed body – that sickly sweet clinging smell, heavy and nasty – that's just what it was like! I'm sorry I can't get nearer than this, but it is most difficult. I think the fact that it was February disproved any idea of "flowering bushes" or fertiliser – and it *wasn't* pig, as since suggested by one of the papers.' There were three other aspects of this strange odour. It was confined to a patch of ground, some three yards long; her companions could walk in, and out, of the affected area. There was a strong wind blowing at the time but, even after the duration of ten minutes, the smell was still present. Intriguingly one of Miss Dudley's companions could smell nothing at all – even though he had indeed a strong sense of smell.

There have been many attempts at explanation or elucidation of the events surrounding the rectory and the church in Borley. It has been calculated that the phenomena connected with the house and garden have been described by over two hundred separate witnesses. It has even been conjectured that the witnesses themselves have been the agents of the unusual activity; unknown to themselves, some force taps their energies. There were many occasions, for example, when events took place while other people were sleeping in the house. This is true of many 'ghost stories'.

Sceptics have doubted the evidence of Borley Rectory, and questioned the motives of those who have provided it. The truth of the matter is now beyond recall. It is perhaps better to conclude with some words of Immanuel Kant on the subject of ghosts – 'while one can be sceptical about any individual instance, the sum total presents a body of evidence that is difficult to ignore'.

Animal spirits

The disappearing dachshund

SPECTRAL DOGS ARE FAMILIAR THROUGHOUT ENGLAND. THEY TEND TO BE black, and hairy. They were known in some regions as 'barghasts'. Suicides, and hanged men, were reputed to come again in that guise, haunting the place of their death. Unbaptised babies also took that form, in order to pursue their offending parents. There was until recent years a Dog Lane at Uplyme, where a spectral dog appeared. Doghill Barrow north of Stonehenge is apparently the lair of a phantom. There is a Black Dog village in Devon. 'The Devil and his Dandy Dogs' were said to run, howling, across the Cornish moors. They were 'Whisht' hounds on Dartmoor and 'Yeth' hounds on Exmoor, the 'Seven Whistlers' in Worcestershire and 'Gabriel Hounds' in the north of England. These hell-hounds are related to the stories of the Wild Hunt that were popular in the early medieval period. From the *Anglo-Saxon Chronicle* for the year 1127 comes the report that after 6 February many people saw and heard a hunting pack in full cry. 'The dogs were as black as pitch with large and staring eyes . . . Throughout the night the monks heard the hunters sounding and blowing their horns.' What strange disorders of the night can prompt these accounts? There is a spectral dog known in East Anglia variously as 'Shuck', 'Shucky Dod' and 'Old Shock', derived from the Anglo-Saxon *scucca* meaning demon.

In a study of Wiltshire ghosts, there is an account of a black dog regularly seen at the hamlet of Quemeford; it has been observed jumping over hedges, and frequenting a certain bridle path. One inhabitant of the hamlet 'saw a black dog with a chain dangling from its collar, which passed him absolutely noiselessly, and went through a closed door'. From Wiltshire, too, comes the following story. 'When first married I lived in a cottage up Fetch Common way. The bedroom had wall cupboards in opposite corners of the room, and something used to pass from one cupboard across to the other. The "thing" was large, dark and animal-like.' There are also accounts of a dog, commonly described as white with red ears. It is believed to presage death. The ghost that brings news of death is known as a 'fetch'. Some dogs are invisible, but their panting can be heard as they walk beside a traveller; these are believed to be friendly guardians. Dogs are, in addition, held to be highly sensitive to unusual activity that human beings construe as ghost-like.

There are accounts of canine spectres less sinister than those of the ubiquitous 'black dog'; two letters were published in 1909, regarding events in the same London street. They were addressed to Elliott O'Donnell, who had recently given a lecture on 'A Future Life for Dumb Animals'. The extract from the first letter is as follows.

'Though I am by no means over-indulgent to dogs, the latter generally greet me very effusively, and it would seem that there is something in my individuality that is peculiarly attractive to them.

'This being so, I was not greatly surprised one day, when in the immediate neighbourhood of W— Street, to be persistently followed by a rough-haired dachshund wearing a gaudy yellow collar. I tried to scare it away by shaking my sun-shade at it, but all to no purpose – it came resolutely on; and I was beginning to despair of getting rid of it when I came to X— Street, where my husband once practised as an oculist. There it suddenly altered its tactics and, instead of keeping at my heels, became my conductor, forging slowly ahead with a gliding motion that both puzzled and fascinated me.

'I, furthermore, observed the temperature – it was a whit not less than ninety degrees in the shade – the legs and stomach of the dachshund were covered with mud and dripping with water. When it came to number 90 it halted, and, veering swiftly round, eyed me in the strangest manner. It remained in this attitude until I was within two or three feet of it – certainly not more – when to my unlimited amazement it absolutely vanished – melted into thin air.

'The iron gate leading to the area was closed, so there was nowhere for it to have hidden and, besides, I was almost bending over at the time, as I wanted to read the name on its collar.

'There being no one near at hand I could not obtain a second opinion, and so came away wondering whether what I had actually seen was a phantasm or a mere hallucination.

'Number 90, I might add, judging by the brass plate on the door, was inhabited by a doctor with an unpronounceable foreign name.'

The second correspondent, unknown to the lady who wrote the first letter, lived in the vicinity of X— Street. One morning her rough-haired dachshund, Robert, disappeared. Searches were made in the neighbourhood, and advertisements were placed in the press, to no avail. Then she goes on to state that

'I was walking along W— Street one evening when, to my intense joy and surprise, I suddenly saw my darling standing on the pavement a few feet ahead of me, regarding me intently from out of his pathetic brown eyes.

'A sensation of extreme coldness now stole over me, and I noticed with something akin to shock that in spite of the hot, dry weather Robert looked as if he had been out in the rain for hours.

'He still wore the bright yellow collar I had bought him shortly before his disappearance, so that had there been any doubt about his identity that would have removed it instantly.

'On my calling to him he turned quickly round and, with a slight gesture of the head as if bidding me to follow, he glided slowly forward. My natural impulse was to run after him, pick him up and smother him in kisses; but try as hard as I would I could not diminish the distance between us, although he never appeared to alter his pace. I was quite out of breath by the time we reached X— Street where, to my surprise, he stopped at number 90 and, turning round again, gazed at me in the most beseeching manner . . . I do not know for how long we stood there looking at one another; it may have been minutes, or hours, or, again, but a few paltry seconds. He took the initiative from me, for as I leaped forward to raise him in my arms, he glided through the closed gateway of number 90 descending the stone steps into the area.

'Convinced now that what I had beheld was Robert's apparition, I determined to see the strange affair through to the bitter end and, entering the gate, I also went down into the area.

'The phantasm had come to an abrupt halt by the side of a low wooden box, and as I foolishly made an abortive attempt to reach it with my hand, it vanished instantaneously.

'I searched the area thoroughly, and was assured that there was no outlet, save by the steps I had just descended, and no hole or nook where anything the size of Robert could be completely hidden from sight.'

Then the correspondent noticed that, in the wooden box where the dog had vanished, there was a piece of raw meat. She ascertained from the plate on the door that the owner of the house was a German doctor and, when she knocked, a German man-servant came to the door. She was told that the doctor saw no one without an appointment and, when she unwisely mentioned the meat in the box, she was asked to leave since the master 'stands no nonsense from anyone'.

She later found out from a medical friend that the doctor in question 'was deemed to be a clever fellow at a certain London hospital, where he was often occupied in vivisection'.

What would it have?

This is a narrative reprinted in George Sinclair's *Satan's Invisible World Discovered*, published in 1685. It concerns the visit to Oxfordshire of the commissioners set up by the 'purged parliament' to administer the affairs of that county under the general leadership of Oliver Cromwell. They are unlikely to have fabricated this account, or wished to be seen as credulous or superstitious in any way. Charles 1 had been executed on 30 January 1649.

'The Commissioners, October 13, 1649, with their Servants being come to the Mannor-house of Woodstock, they took up their lodging in the King's own Rooms; the Bed-Chamber and the Withdrawing Room: the former whereof, they also make their Kitchin, and the Council-Hall their brewhouse; the Chamber of Presence, their place of sitting to dispatch business, and a wood-house of the Dining Room, where they laid the wood of that ancient Standard in the High Park, known by all, of the name of the Kings Oak which (that nothing might remain that had the name of King affixed to it) they digged up by the Roots.

'October 14 and 15 they had little disturbance: but on the 16 there came as they thought into the Bed-Chamber, where two of the Commissioners and their Servants lay, the shape of a Dog which going under their Beds did, as it were, gnaw their Bed-cords. But on the morrow finding them whole, and a quarter of Beef, which lay on the ground, untouched, they began to entertain other thoughts.

'October 17. Something to their thinking removed all the Wood of the Kings Oak out of the Dining Room into the Presence Chamber, and hurled the Chairs and Stools up and down that Room. From whence it came into the two Chambers, where the Commissioners and their Servants lay, and hoysted up their Beds-feet so much higher than their heads, that they thought they should have been turned over and over: and then let them fall down with such a force, that their bodies rebounded from the bed a good distance, and then shook the Bedsteads so violently, that they themselves confest that their Bodies were sore with it.

'October 18. Something came into the Bed-Chamber, and walkt up and down, and fetching the Warming-pan out of the Withdrawing Room, made so much noise that they thought five Bells could not have made more.

'And October 19. Trenchers [plates cut from stale bread] were thrown up and down the Dining Room and at them who lodged thereof, whereof one of them being wakned, put forth his head to see what was the matter, but had Trenchers thrown at it.

'October 20. The Curtains of the Bed in the Withdrawing Room were drawn to and fro, and the Bedsteads much shaken, and eight great Pewter-Dishes, and three dozen of Trenchers thrown about the Bed-Chamber again. This night they also thought whole armfuls of the Wood of the Kings Oak, were thrown down in their Chambers, but of that in the morning they found nothing had been moved.

'October 21. The Keeper of their Ordinary [kitchen], and his Bitch, lay in one of the Rooms with them, which night they were not disturbed at all. But October 22 though the Bitch kennelled there again, to whom they ascribed their former nights rest, both they and the Bitch were in a pitiful taking, the Bitch opening but once and that with a whining fearful yelp.

'October 23. They had all their cloaths pluckt off them in the Withdrawing Room, and the Bricks fell out of the Chimney into the Room. And on the 24 they thought in the Dining Room that all the Wood of the Kings Oak had been brought thither, and thrown down close by their Bed-side; which being heard by those of the Withdrawing Room, one of them rose to see what was done, fearing indeed that his Fellow-Commissioners had been killed, but found no such matter; whereupon returning to his Bed again, he found two or three dozen of Trenchers thrown into it, and handsomely covered with the Bed-cloaths.

'October 25. The Curtains of the Bed in the Withdrawing Room were drawn to and fro, and the Bed-stead shaken as before, and in the Bed-Chamber glass flew about so thick (and yet not one lozenge of the Chamber windows broken) that they thought it had rained money. Whereupon they lighted Candles, but to their grief they found nothing but glass.

'October 29. Something going to the window opened and shut it: then going into the Bed-Chamber it threw great stones, for half an hours time, some whereof lighted on the High-bed, others on the Truckle-bed, to the number in all above four score. This night here was also a very great noise, as if forty Piece of Ordinance had been shot off together. During these noises which were heard in both Rooms together, both Commissioners and their Servants were struck with so great horror, that they cryed out to one another for help; whereof one of them recovering himself out of a strange Agony he had been in, snatchd a Sword and had like to have killed one of his Brethren coming out of his Bed in his Shirt, which he took for the

Spirit that did all the mischief. However at length they got all together, yet the Noise continued so great and terrible, and shook the Walls so much, that they thought the whole Mannor would have fallen on their Heads. At its departure it took all the Glass of the Windows away with it.

'November 1. Something as they thought walkt up and down the Withdrawing Room, and then made a noise in the Dining Room. The stones which were left before, and laid up in the Withdrawing Room, were all fetcht away this night, and a great deal of Glass (not like the former) thrown about again.

'November 2. There came something into the Withdrawing Room, treading as they conceived much like a Bear, which first only walked about a quarter of an hour: at length it made a noise about the Table, and threw the Warming-pan so violently that it quite spoiled it. It threw also a Glass and great Stones at them again; and the bones of Horses, and all so violently that the Bed-stead and the Walls were bruised by them. This night they planted Candles all about the Rooms, and made fires up to the Rantle-trees of the Chimneys, but all were put out, no Body knew how, the Fire and Burn-wood which made it, being thrown up and down the Rooms, the Curtains torn with the Rods from their Beds, and the Bed-posts pulled away, that the Tester fell down upon them, and the feet of the Bed-stead cloven into two. And upon the Servants in the Truckle-bed, who lay all the time sweating for fear; there was first a little, which made them begin to stir, but before they could get out a whole Tub full, as it were of stinking Ditch-water down upon them, so green that it made their Shirts and Sheets of that colour too. The same night the Windows were all broke by throwing of Stones, and there was most terrible noises in three several places together to the extraordinary wonder of all that lodged near them. Nay the very Rabbit Stealers who were abroad that night were so affrighted with the dismal

Thundering that for haste they left their Ferrets in the holes, behind them, beyond Rosamonds Well. Notwithstanding all this one of them had the boldness to ask, in the Name of GOD, what it was, what it would have, and what they had done, that they should be disturbed after this manner? To which no answer was given but it ceased for a while . . .

'Then began violent Noises again, insomuch that they calling to one another, got together, and went into the Presence Chamber, where they said Prayers and sang Psalms, notwithstanding all which the Thundering still continued in other Rooms. After this, November 3, they removed to their Lodgings over the Gate; and next day being Sunday went to Ewelm, where, how they escaped, the Authors of the Relation knew not. But returning on Monday the Devil (for that was the name they gave their nightly Guest) left them not unvisited, nor on the Tuesday following, which was the last day they stayed.'

The bear

Richard Baxter, author of *The Certainty of the World of Spirits* (1691), has this anecdote.

'*Simon Jones*, a Strong and healthful Man of *Kederminster* (no way inclined to Melancholy or any Fancies) hath oft told me, that being a Souldier for the King in the War against the Parliament, in a clear Moon-shine Night, as he stood Sentinel in the Colledge Green at *Worcester*, something like a headless Bear appeared to him; and so affrighted him, that he laid down his Arms soon after, and returned home to his Trade.'

Moving things

Poltergeist

THE ACTIVITY GIVEN THE NAME OF 'POLTERGEIST' IS SO WELL KNOWN
and so frequently attested that it may seem unnecessary to detail
its particular manifestations. But a brief summary may prove useful.
The activity generally begins with 'knocking' or 'rapping' in certain
rooms, as if something were trying to announce its presence. Then
characteristically there follow louder or more frightening noises such
as the thumping on floors and walls or the sounds of scratching.
These in turn tend to be followed by noises as of furniture being
thrown violently around a room that can increase in frequency and
intensity within a matter of days or weeks. In one recent case there
was heard the distinct noise of someone 'grinding his boot heel in a
scattering of grit or gravel'.

Only after the stage of sound has been passed is there evidence
of actual movement. Pieces of furniture seem to shift of their own
accord. Doors are flung open or violently closed. The drawers of
cupboards also open and close of their own volition. Plates are
smashed. Light bulbs explode or flicker uncontrollably. This activity
can then be followed by the witnessing of objects being thrown into
the air, apparently of their own accord. The curious thing is that if

these objects strike a human being they generally inflict no injury. But if they strike inanimate objects they can cause damage.

There is the curious phenomenon, attested in some cases, of the sudden and inexplicable appearance of water. So we have a report from 1893 on the haunting of the Buckley household. There had been sounds of heavy steps, and other characteristic signals, but when 'Miss Buckley was in the attic, kneeling by a trunk, she felt some water "switched" at her. She thought it was a practical joke of her brother's, but he was not in the room. A small pool of water was on the floor where she stood, and the wall beyond was sprinkled. Soon after, as Mr Buckley went upstairs in the dark, carrying an ink-bottle and some pens, he found his hand wet. He thought it must be ink, but on getting to the light found that it was clear water; there was a little pool of water on the stair where this occurred, but no sign of damp on the ceiling above.' Some time later, a figure of a woman appeared in the house. There were reports of a haunting in Stow-on-the-Wold, in 1963, for which the dripping or oozing of water was evidence. The water ran down the bedroom walls of the house in question, and dripped through the ceiling of the lounge to such an extent that the furniture and carpets had to be covered. Bowls were placed over the floor to catch the drops as they came down. There was nothing wrong with the plumbing of the house. Two months later the first messages appeared on scraps of paper. Events such as these have occurred through the centuries.

A thirteenth-century poem, in the *South East Legendary*, records how the harp of St Dunstan played itself just before the saint's death:

The harpe song al bi hire-self: as heo henk bi the walle.

This is one of the earliest accounts of poltergeist activity.

We have this narrative from the early seventeenth century of disturbances in the house of Peter Pain, a shoemaker of Mary Poel

Street in Bristol. Mr Pain 'was extreamly disturbed with most surprizing and unaccountable noises for some time; and one night above the rest, about 12 of the Clock, the usual noise was accompanied by so great a light throughout the whole House, as if every Room had been full of burning Tapers, or Torches; These repeated scenes of Horrour so amazed the whole Family that they applied themselves to the then Minister of St Nicholas who was easily prevailed withal to visit the House; which he no sooner entred, but he became an Earwitness of the most dreadful and unaccustomed noises; so, together with the whole Family, he repaired into a Chamber at one end of the Gallery, at the other end of which, was a large bulky Trunk, full of old lumber, and so heavy, that four or five men were not able to lift it: Having shut the door to them, the Minister went to Prayers, during part of which time the noise continued, and on a sudden something was flung against the Chamber door, with extraordinary violence, upon which the noise immediately ceased. When Prayer was ended, they went to go forth of the Chamber door, but could by no means force it open, until they had called for the assistance of some of the Neighbours, who running in to their relief, found the door barr'd close with the great Trunk aforesaid; upon which they all concluded that it was cast there in that violent manner, when they heard that mighty shock against the door, just before the ceasing of the noise . . . the whole Transaction is still recent in the memories of the Neighbours, who were Witnesses of the amazing Troubles, which at that time disturbed the house.'

Here is another account from the seventeenth century. 'There is a farm in Burton, a village in the parish of Weobley, which Mr William Bridges, a linen draper of London, has in mortgage from one Thomas Tomkyns, a decayed yeoman. This farm was taken in by lease of Mrs Elizabeth Bridges, about Michaelmas 1669. Soon after this tenant was entered on the farm, some familiar began to act apish pranks by knocking boldly at the door in the dark of the evening, and the like early in the morning, but nobody to be seen. The stools and forms [benches] were thrown into disorder, heaps of malt and vetches mingled, a mow of pulse and pease likewise; loaves of bread on a table carried into another room, or hid in tubs covered with cloths; cabbage plants dug up and replanted in various patterns; a half-roasted pig demolished except for the bones; some cattle died and among others a sow leaped up and danced in strange postures, and at last fell down dead.'

In 1646 a house in Lutterworth was strangely disturbed. 'Multitudes flockt to see it and affirmed, that at a certain hour of the day, stones were thrown at those that were present, which hit them but hurt them not. And that what ever time any one would whistle, it was answered by a whistle in the Room. And no search could discover any Fraud.' The report appeared in Richard Baxter's *The Certainty of the World of Spirits*, from which compendium the following story is taken. 'Mr Mun, rector of Stockerston in Leicestershire, had a Daughter married to one Mr Beecham, rector of Braunston in Rutland; in whose House it was frequently observed that a Tobacco-pipe would move itself from off a Shelf at one end of the Room, to another Shelf at the other end of the Room, without any Hand. Mr Mun, visiting his son-in-law, took a Pipe of Tobacco in that Room, and looked for some such Motion; but a great Bible, instead of a Pipe, moved itself off from a Desk at the lower end of the Room, and cast itself into his Lap . . . I have no reason to suspect the Veracity of a sober Man, a constant Preacher and a good Scholar.'

From the eighteenth century come stories of 'the cold lad of Hylton', a poltergeist of Hylton Castle in Sunderland. He was rarely seen, but he was heard nightly by the servants. 'If the kitchen had been left in perfect order, they heard him amusing himself by hurling the pewter in all directions, and throwing everything into confusion. If on the contrary the apartment had been left in disarray (a practice which the servants found it both prudent and convenient to adopt) the indefatigable goblin arranged everything with the nicest precision.'

There is this report from the nineteenth century. 'Some time since, a gentleman having established himself in a lodging in London, felt, the first night he slept there, that the clothes [sheets and blankets] were being dragged off his bed. He fancied he had done it himself in his sleep, and pulled them on again; but it happens repeatedly: he gets out of bed each time – can find nobody, no string, no possible explanation – nor can obtain any from the people in the house, who only seem distressed and annoyed. On mentioning it to someone in the neighbourhood, he is informed that the same thing has occurred to several preceding occupants of the lodging which, of course, he left.' The report of bed-clothes being removed or disturbed is a common one.

There is a case from what was then the little village of Wem in Shropshire, reported in the newspapers of November 1883. The first manifestation occurred in a farmhouse, known as 'Woods', about ten miles from Shrewsbury. I take up the account from Andrew Lang's *Book of Dreams and Ghosts*. 'First a saucepan full of eggs "jumped" off the fire in the kitchen, and the tea-things, leaping from the table, were broken. Cinders were "thrown out of the fire", and set some clothes in a blaze. A globe leaped off a lamp. A farmer, Mr Lea, saw all the windows of the upper storey "as it were on fire", but it was no such matter. The nursemaid ran out in a fright, to a neighbour's, and her dress spontaneously combusted as she ran. The people attributed these and similar events to something in the coal, or in the air, or to electricity. When the nurse-girl, Emma Davies, sat on the lap of the schoolmistress Miss Maddox, her boots kept flying off . . .' It was reported in the *Daily News* that this young girl, Emma Davies, had confessed her responsibility for all these events, but then Emma herself denied making the confession. It seems to be yet another case when genuine activity is assisted by human intervention. The other servants swore that they saw crockery rise by itself from the kitchen table. One servant, Priscilla, 'also saw crockery come out of a cupboard, in detachments, and fly between her and Emma, usually in a slanting direction, while Emma stood by with her arms folded'.

There are often stray reports and brief references to what would seem to have been poltergeist activity. In nineteenth-century records we come across allusions, for example, to 'a haunted house between Hinton and Crewkerne. The people who lived there before the ones who do now used to have their weaving press moved.' Of another house, in Chink just outside Ilminster, it was said that 'things used to get thrown about. It used to torment the place, and clothes put down at night would not be there next day. The last people gave up in desperation, and the place was turned into a cattle stall.' The detail of the cattle stall lends authenticity to the account.

The gamekeeper of Lord Portman, Mr Newman, gave a sworn statement on 23 January 1895. He said that he saw a boot come flying out of a door. 'I went and put a foot on the boot and said, "I defy anything to move this boot." Just as I stepped off, it rose up behind me and knocked my hat off. There was nobody behind me.'

There are many twentieth-century accounts, some of which have been included in this book. Of a place known only as Wood Court it was reported that 'the poker jumps in the grate, and one night the light started to swing round and round for no reason. They were playing cards late into the night and the visitors, strangers in the services, were scared out of their wits, and lost their concentration, and did badly at cards. The front and back doors were kept open wide by the previous owner to allow the spirit easy access in and out of the house.'

Graham J. McEwan, in his *Haunted Churches of England*, reports the testimony of Mrs Joyce Bennett. She worked as a nurse at St Osyth's convalescent home near Clacton-on-Sea in Essex; it lies on the site of an ancient priory, and seems to have been the centre of many unusual disturbances over the years. On one occasion in 1977 Mrs Bennett was in the nursing office, while one of the cleaning staff was working outside. The woman called to her to 'come quickly'. 'Thinking a patient had become ill,' she said, 'I ran from the room, to find her staring at the carpet on the landing. She told me that the carpet had been trying to throw her up against the wall. I laughed and told her that the carpet could not move and demonstrated how it was fixed. I was about to turn and walk away, when the carpet, to my amazement, moved quickly and the cleaner was thrown, just as she had said, up against the wall. After this incident she left and never returned. This, it transpired, had happened on two previous occasions, despite the carpet being apparently securely fixed to the floor.'

It is curious that poltergeist activity is often associated with the presence of young girls of twelve or thirteen years. Some were diagnosed with hysteria or what was known in the sixteenth century as 'the mother'. In one celebrated case, reported in 1895, the noises and disturbances followed a girl when she changed house. This in turn would suggest that these girls are in some unknown or indefinable way 'causing' the activity. We might conclude, therefore, that objects rise into the air or are hurled about, thunderous noises are provoked, and doors violently slammed shut, by human agency. If there are forms of energy that can indeed be responsible for phenomena that seem to defy natural laws, is it possible that human beings in some way create the 'ghosts' that are the subject of this book? Are we dealing with unknown powers of the living rather than of the dead?

The carpenters

THE MOTHER OF GEORGE CANNING, THE EARLY NINETEENTH-CENTURY Prime Minister, had previously earned her living as a relatively obscure stage actress. But, as a result of her illustrious son, her story of a haunting became well known. At an early stage of her career she found employment at a theatre in Portsmouth where the manager, Mr Bernard, had found for her lodgings at a very low rate. 'I have a house,' he told her, 'belonging to our carpenter that is reported to be haunted, and nobody will live in it. If you like to have it, you may, and for nothing, I believe, for he is so anxious to get a tenant; only you must not let it be known that you do not pay rent for it.'

Mrs Hunn (that was her name at this time) was well acquainted with the stories of theatrical ghosts that sit in the upper circle or haunt certain 'green rooms'; they are even meant to bring good luck to any production at which they are seen. So she assured Mr Bernard that she was not in the least disturbed by the reputation of the house. Her luggage was brought, followed by her children and by a young maid. When the maid and children had retired to bed, she lit two candles in her own chamber and in the spirit of curiosity stayed up to witness the appearance of any spirit. Beneath the room she occupied was the workshop of the carpenter itself. This workshop had two doors, one leading to the street and the other leading into the passage of the house; the street door was barred and bolted, while the door to the passage was on the latch. All was quiet.

She had been reading a book for a while when she became aware of a sound issuing from the workshop that was very much like the sawing of wood. Then other noises began to accompany this sound – among them knocking and hammering and planing. It was as if half a dozen carpenters were in busy employment. Mrs Hunn was of a bold disposition and, wishing to discover more, took off her shoes and quietly descended the stairs with a lighted candle in her hand. The noises of work continued as she came down into the hallway; but then, when she unlatched the door and went into the workshop, all was silent and still. None of the tools had been touched. None of the wood had been moved. Having examined every part of the room she went back to her own room, beginning to doubt the evidence of her senses in this matter. But, after she had entered the room, the noises of sawing and hammering began again and continued for approximately half an hour. When they ceased she went to bed. She had decided to tell no one about her experience but, instead, to listen the next night for any unusual sounds.

On the following night they began again, just as before. So she confided in Mr Bernard, who agreed to watch with her on the next night. The noises commenced once more but, instead of entering the workshop as she wished him to do, he rushed horrified into the street. Mrs Hunn herself occupied these lodgings for the rest of the summer and, having become familiar with the strange sounds below her, was not at all ill at ease. In fact, as she said later, 'if they had stopped, I would have been afraid. I might have feared that the carpenters would visit me upstairs.'

Fly like lightning

On 20 or 21 February 1883 Mrs White was washing up the tea things in the kitchen of her cottage in Worksop, with two of her children, when to her surprise the wooden table tilted upwards at a considerable angle. That was the first phenomenon. On 1 March 1883, Mrs White was in the company of a girl, Eliza Rose; Eliza Rose was the child of an 'imbecile mother', and spent much of her time with the Whites. It was said that the girl was 'half-witted', but there is no evidence of that. At about 11.30 on the evening of that day a large number of objects, previously seen in the kitchen, came tumbling down the stairs. They were subsequently followed by hot coals. On the following night, when Mr White was in the kitchen with his wife and with Eliza, a host of household objects came flying down the stairs. Mr White, of course, rushed upstairs, but found nothing out of order. When he came back into the kitchen, a small china figurine left the mantelpiece and flew into a corner of the room. When Mr White put it back in its accustomed place, it repeated its flight into the corner.

At this point a doctor, Doctor Lloyd, and a priest, the Reverend Higgs, were summoned to the cottage. These two gentlemen witnessed a basin and cream-jug rising from the floor of their own accord before they fell back and broke. Other objects flew about the room. On the following morning a bedroom clock that had been silent for eighteen months was heard to strike; then there was a crash and, on investigation, it was discovered that the clock had somehow leapt over the bed and fallen onto the floor. Throughout that day, in fact, common household objects were hurled about the room without any visible agency. On another occasion Mr White saw a salt-cellar fly from the kitchen table when Eliza Rose was in another part of the room. When Eliza had left the house to pick up the early witnesses, he saw inanimate objects fly about the room. When she finally departed, to be with her mother, all the phenomena ceased.

In April 1883 an investigator, Mr Podmore, was called in to examine the evidence for, and to interview the witnesses of, these apparently inexplicable events. He reported at the time that 'it may be stated generally that there was no possibility, in most cases, of the objects having been thrown by hand . . . Moreover it is hard to conceive by what mechanical appliance, under the circumstances described, the movements could have been effected . . . To suppose that these various objects were all moved by mechanical contrivances argues incredible stupidity, amounting almost to imbecility on the part of all the persons present who were not in the plot.' The Reverend Higgs testified that 'the jar did not or could not go in a straight line from the cupboard out of the door; but it certainly did go'.

There has been no convincing explanation for the events here related.

*

A REPORT IN THE *RETFORD, WORKSOP AND GAINSBOROUGH NEWS* OF 10 March 1883 is of some interest.

'The town of Worksop was in an uproar on Saturday (March 3, 1883) consequent on the circulation of a report that the household goods of a man named Joseph Wright, a well-known dealer, were being smashed and removed by some unknown agency. All day long crowds of excited people wended their way towards the New Building Ground, where White's semi-detached house stands, drawn thither by the accounts of the mysterious occurrences said to have been witnessed by the inmates and others.

'As I entered the door I myself saw an Oxford frame slip out of the rocking chair. I told the boy to pick it up; and he said he dare not. After hearing what the folks had to say, I was joining in the conversation, when a basin which had stood on the meal-bin began to rise in a slanting direction over my head and then fell at my feet, smashing into bits. I had not the slightest belief in the supernatural. I cannot account for what I saw. No one was nearer to the basin than myself and, as far as I saw, there was no cause for the phenomenon. The room was dimly lighted by a candle.

'We were talking about the things, and the doctor was saying, "It is a very mysterious thing", with his back turned to the flour bin, when a basin which stood on the bin suddenly flew up slantingly over the doctor's head, to where some bacon was hanging on some hooks, and fell down and smashed at his feet. The doctor looked in the bin, and found nothing, and thinking the devil was in the place, he left and went home. About half-a-dozen people were in the room whilst these things happened.

'I followed Mr White into another room, and he called my attention to the bare walls, saying that everything except the clock and a stuffed pigeon in a glass case, which remained on their respective nails, had been dashed to the ground and broken. The clock hung over the bed, which was right up in the corner of the room, with the head and one side close to the walls. While White was telling me that the chest of drawers before us had been turned topsy-turvy, we heard a smash and on turning my head I saw the clock in the middle of the floor with its end knocked out. I was the nearest person to the clock when it hung on the wall.

'The servant girl opened the door of the room, and came inside just as the clock left the wall. If White or the servant had been instrumental in throwing the clock down, I could not have failed to detect them. We went back into the kitchen, and I stood looking towards the fire, with the girl on my left hand engaged in some domestic duty, and White on my right hand, I saw a pot-dog ornament, such a one as you see in old people's houses, smash on the floor in front of me. It had come off the mantelpiece, but I did not see it leave the mantelpiece. The things seemed to fly like lightning, and you only knew they were gone when you saw them broken on the floor. I picked up the broken dog, and closely examined it; but I saw no string or spring on it. Then I saw a cream-jug, which had stood on the table, jump to the floor and smash. The brass candlesticks next flew off the mantelpiece, going towards the back door. Everything flew towards the door. I cannot account for the occurrences; and if I had not seen for myself I should not have believed that the removal of articles could have taken place in the way that it did.

'White and his family, with the exception of his wife, agree in laying all the blame on the shoulders of the unfortunate girl, alleging that she had "overlooked" the house; but all agree in attributing the spiritual demonstration to powers higher than human.

'Our representative on Monday evening interviewed the girl, Rose. She says she is eighteen years old; but she is very small, and looks to be not more than fifteen, while physically she appears quite incapable of being the cause of the extraordinary occurrences which have taken place; nor is there anything in her manner to induce anyone to think she could concoct and carry out such trickery. All sorts of theories are put forward to account for the occurrences – galvanic batteries, animal magnetism; while some incomprehensible mediums are mentioned as causes by the ignorant, who know not that glass and earthenware are non-conductors of electricity.'

The Enfield affair

In the mid-1970s Mrs Peggy Harper and her four children moved into a semi-detached council house in Enfield, north London. The events, which were widely reported and verified at the time, began in the summer of 1977. One night in the August of that year two of her children, Janet and Peter, came to tell their mother that their beds had been moving. On going into their room, she found nothing out of order. On the next night the children complained of a shuffling or scraping noise in their bedroom. It sounded to them as if the chair were being moved, or as if someone were shuffling across the floor in slippers. Peggy Harper removed the chair from the room. When she turned the light off, however, she herself heard the sound. She turned on the light, and the noise stopped. She turned off the light, and the sound of scraping began again.

The phenomena soon increased in intensity. Four loud knocks against the wall were heard, by the neighbours as well as by the Harpers. A chest of drawers moved approximately eighteen inches from the wall. Peggy pushed it back again. When she turned away the chest of drawers moved out again, and proved impossible to return to its original position. The drawers in the chest also came out, and could not be moved. Peggy, now thoroughly alarmed, took the children and left the house to take refuge with neighbours. The police were called to investigate the phenomena. The officers also heard the knocking on the walls, and in a signed statement one of them testified that he had seen a chair move of its own accord across the floor. On the next day the family were plagued by a rain of flying objects, including marbles and toy bricks, which were hot to the touch.

The news of the phenomena spread into the local and the national press. Witnesses – among them the local vicar as well as numerous reporters and police officers – testified to the incidents of unexplained noises and of objects being hurled about the room. Puddles of water appeared on the floor. The sheets and blankets were torn off the sleeping children. One investigator, who spent some fourteen months on the case, was alarmed one morning when he heard a very loud vibration in another room as if a hole were being drilled through the wall. He went into the bedroom and saw that a Victorian fireplace had been ripped from its casing and hurled upon the floor. It weighed some sixty pounds, and could not have been removed by the children.

At one point Janet Harper began to speak in a rasping male voice, claiming to be 'Bill' who had died in the house. 'I had a haemorrhage,' he said, 'and then I fell asleep and died in a chair in the corner downstairs.' None of the Harper farmily knew that, many years ago, a 'Bill' Wilkins had indeed died in the house while sitting in a chair in the living room. There are also reports of Janet being dragged across the floor, and two witnesses concur in the sight of her levitating above her bed.

Of course Janet herself came under suspicion for manufacturing the evidence. It soon became clear that, in her absence, the phenomena ceased. It is indeed possible that, given the excitement of the publicity, the young girl did indeed collude with the source of the phenomena.

But it is difficult to account for the chest of drawers or for the moving furniture as witnessed by others. This would not be the first occasion when a human subject – generally a young girl – has some connection, wilful or otherwise, with what is generally considered to be poltergeist activity. In a television documentary, made at the end of 2007, Janet Harper explained that 'I'm not sure the poltergeist was truly "evil". It was almost as if he wanted to be part of our family. It didn't want to hurt us.' She admitted to manufacturing a few hoaxes, but explained that she did so out of frustration with the researchers. In any case she insisted that she was responsible for only 1 or 2 per cent of the phenomena. After two years, all of the disturbances stopped.

The Runcorn mystery

IN THE MONTHS OF AUGUST AND SEPTEMBER 1952, A HOUSE IN RUNCORN, Cheshire, became a centre of unusual activities that have generally been explained as the manifestation of a poltergeist. Mr Sam Jones had lived at 1, Byron Street, Runcorn, for some thirty-three years; in the house, too, were his daughter-in-law and his grandson called John Glynn. A female lodger, Miss Ellen Whittle, was also in residence. The small house was on the corner of the street, at the end of a row of similar such houses or cottages. The occurrences began on Sunday 17 August 1952. The police were called, in the hope that they might be able to detect a hoaxer, but no such individual was found. A police sergeant reported that John Glynn was in a state of 'nervous collapse'. Much against the wishes of the people directly concerned, the events in Byron Street began to be reported in the press at the end of August.

The local Methodist minister, the Reverend W. H. Stevens, read the accounts and became immediately intrigued by the intensity of the phenomena. He visited Byron Street on Monday 22 September. A crowd had gathered outside the house. As he was a Methodist minister he was allowed to remain in the house for the duration of the evening and night. He entered the grandson's room a little after 11.30; John

Glynn had retired there, and had asked a friend to sleep with him in the iron double bedstead to 'inspire courage'. While the Reverend Stevens stood there the dressing table creaked loudly and began to move of its own accord; then it began to shake and rock. Stevens pushed it back into a corner and, on his extinguishing his torch, it began to rock and move. Someone switched on the electric light, so that Stevens and other witnesses behind him saw the shaking table with no one near it.

One local businessman, J. C. Davies, was standing behind the Reverend Stevens on this occasion. He reported that 'to my great astonishment the dresser continued in full light [a 100-watt lamp and three torches] to beat itself against the wall rocking *violently*. This, I imagine, continued for three seconds at least, and certainly there was no possibility of physical contact from the bed. I then tried to turn this furniture with my foot, but this was quite impossible.' It was also recorded that the movement of the dressing table was so intense that plaster fell down from the ceiling below.

The two boys were lying in the bed, wrapped up in their sheets. Then certain articles from the dressing table were sent flying across the room. Mr Davies went on to say that 'books and torches, a clock, ornaments, pillows etcetera in the darkness began to fly about'.

Reverend Stevens has left his own report of the incident. 'A small alarm clock, books, one book striking me gently on the head. A table runner, about five feet in length of thin cotton material, was ripped from top to bottom in one movement. A drawer was flung out and its contents fell on the bed. A heavy box between the beds struck the single bed and later turned over with a bang.' It is noticeable that the book struck him gently. Mr Davies had noticed that 'when these missiles hit *people* no serious hurt was done. Often, however, these objects hit walls or doors and great scars were afterwards visible, in some cases penetrating plaster to the brick-work.'

On another occasion the Reverend Stevens pushed the dressing table against a wall, and placed some objects (including two books and a jigsaw) upon it. Standing in the dark, beside the dressing table, he became aware that 'the contents of the table began to hurl themselves across the room. Eventually I heard the two books fly across, then the rattle of the jigsaw in the box. This was what I was waiting for and straight away I shone my torch. The jigsaw was travelling across the room rising about seven feet in the air. The boys were well covered in the clothes in the exact position as they had been when the light had been switched off.' Mr Davies, on another visit to the house, reported that the lights of the bedroom were suddenly switched on at a prearranged signal and 'I distinctly saw in excellent light a cardboard box almost in suspension above the bed'.

Another interested visitor, Harold Crowther, a local farmer, also visited the boys' bedroom. He put his overcoat on the dressing table and remarked, 'If you don't want it, give it back to me.' It was thrown back to him three times in succession.

Another Methodist minister, the Reverend J. L. Stafford, was called in to help quieten the phenomena. Fearing trickery he asked John Glynn to sit in a chair in a corner of the room, away from the dressing table. He and a companion then held the boy so that he could not move. The dressing table then began to shake and rock violently, and the movement then passed into a blanket chest.

These untoward events continued throughout September 1952, but then ceased in the following month. By curious chance the lodger in the house, Miss Whittle, accidentally fell into a quarry on the night of 22 October; she died on the following day.

Dust and dirt

IN THE LATE SEVENTEENTH CENTURY EVENTS OF A STRIKING NATURE occurred 'at or near the House of *Joseph Cruttenden*' in Brightling, Sussex, and were recorded in Richard Baxter's *The Certainty of the World of Spirits* (1691).

One Monday night 'as the Man and Woman lay in Bed, Dirt and Dust etcetera was thrown at them, but they could not tell whence it came: They rise and Pray, during which that Disturbance ceases; they went to Bed again, but finding the same trouble they are forced to rise. *Tuesday* about Noon, Dust, Dirt, and several things, are thrown at them again; before Night, a part of an end of their House Fired; they rake it down, it flashes somewhat like Gunpowder; as they stopt it there it began in another place, and thence to another, till the whole House was burnt down. The House, tho' it burnt down to the Ground, it flamed not: The Night was spent in carrying Goods, or one thing or other, from one place to another; they, I think, remaining mostly without Doors. *Thursday*, Colonel *Busbridge* (whose House the former was), being acquainted with the Man's sad Accident, bid them go into another of his Houses in the Parish, whither, when the Goods were brought, such like Disturbances were there also; the House fireth, endeavours are made by many to quench it, but in vain, till the Goods are thrown out, when it ceased with little or no help. In this condition none durst let them into their Doors; they abide under a Hut, the Goods are thrown upside down, Pewter-dishes, Knives, Brickbats strike them, but hurt them not; Mr *Bennett* and Mr *Bradshaw*, Ministers, came to pray with them, when a Knife glanced by the Breast of Mr Bennett, a Bowl or Dish thrown at his Back, but while at Prayers quiet; they were without Doors, there being very many present, a Wooden Tut [small seat] came flying out of the Air, seen by many, and came and struck the Man; as likewise a Horseshoe, which was by some laid away, and it was observ'd of its own accord to rise again and fly to the Man, and strook him in the midst of a hundred People.'

The narration concludes with the following paragraph on the fate of the unhappy couple. ''Tis said they are in a Barn or Alehouse; while they lay without Doors, the Woman sending some Meal to a Neighbours to make Bread, they could not make it up into Loaves, but it was like Butter, and so they put it into the Oven, but it would not bake, but came out as it went in. This Relation came from Mr Collins, who was an Eye-witness of much of it.'

The drummer of Tedworth

In the middle of April 1661, Mr Mompesson came back to his family at Tedworth in Wiltshire after an absence of a few days in London; immediately after his return his wife told him that, while he had been away, she had been plagued by extraordinary noises resounding through the house that she believed to be the work of thieves. He dismissed her complaint as being nothing other than the result of an over-active imagination or perhaps an overworked digestion. Then, three nights later, he heard the noises for himself. He heard a 'very great din and knocking' at the doors and on the outside of the walls of the house.

He immediately arose, dressed himself, and took out a pair of pistols. He truly believed that there was an intruder in the grounds. But as he walked downstairs the noise seemed always to travel before or behind him. When he came to the front door, from which he thought the principal noise had come, there was no one there. Then he heard the knocking at another door. He searched the house but, finding nothing, returned to his bed. As soon as he had retired the noises began again, even more furiously than before, and he heard what he described as 'a thumping and drumming on the top of his house, and then by degrees going off into the air'. This strange hollow noise visited the family very frequently, usually for five nights and then ceased for three nights before beginning again.

There was in fact a drum in the house. It had been confiscated by Mr Mompesson, acting as a magistrate, from an itinerant drummer who was found to be wandering through the countryside with a forged permit. He had kept the drum while he made further enquiries.

The noises did not stop, coming to the house just as the family prepared itself for bed. Then the entity, if that is what it was, came after the youngest children. It beat and shook their bedstead with great force. The children were not aware of any blows, but they were perceived to tremble violently. After this the family would hear the sound of scraping under the bed, and the children would be raised a few inches into the air. It seemed then that the noisy apparition was only interested in them. So the children were removed to the attic or 'cock-loft' in the house, from which no sound had ever issued.

On 1 November it ascended into the attic, making a 'mighty' noise. A young male servant, going into that room one morning, saw two wooden boards of the floor begin to move. He held out his hands and one of the boards was thrust towards him. He shoved it back, and again it was returned to him. This happened apparently twenty times in succession, by which stage other people had entered the room and seen the tussle between the servant and the uninvited guest, who had become known as 'the troubler'. The minister of the local church was summoned, together with other parishioners. The minister prayed beside the bed of the children, but his prayer was followed by extraordinary activity. In the words of a contemporary, 'the Chairs walkt about the Room of themselves, the Childrens shoes were hurled over their head, and every loose thing moved about the Chamber'. A bed-staff was thrown at the minister himself, and hit him on the leg, but it struck him so softly that he scarcely felt it.

The staff stopped just where it fell, without rolling or stirring from the spot.

At the latter end of December the Mompesson family heard a noise like 'the gingling of Money' all over the house. On Christmas Eve one of the sons was 'bit' on his heel by the latch of the door; the pin was so small that it was difficult to pick it out of the boy's flesh. Then one of Mr Mompesson's servants became the victim of this peculiar force. For several nights something tried to pluck off his bed-sheets; sometimes they were in fact taken from him, and shoes were thrown at his head. There were other occasions when he found himself to be forcibly held down. One night the servant, John, became aware of a rustling noise in his chamber and something came across to his bedside 'as if it had been one in Silk'.

At the beginning of January 1662 the family heard 'singing' in the chimney, and from time to time lights were to be seen in various parts of the house. It was a curious fact that during these manifest-ations the dogs of the household could not be persuaded to move. One night 'something was heard coming up the stairs, as if it had been one without shoes'. A door was opened and closed frequently in the children's bedroom and they heard the noise 'as if half a dozen had entered together'. Just before dawn, on 10 January, a drum was heard beating outside Mr Mompesson's bedchamber; then the sound travelled to the other end of the house. Of course the magistrate remembered the itinerant drummer.

There were other noises. Mr Mompesson rushed down the stairs, hearing sounds in the children's rooms, when he heard a voice crying out, 'A Witch, a Witch.' Beneath the bed of the children there came the sound of something 'panting like a Dog out of breath'. Other people came into the room and were aware of what was called at the time 'a bloomy noisome'. Suddenly the chamber became very hot, although there was no fire. The panting and scratching continued under the bed for an hour and a half, the sounds coming back for three nights in a row.

One observer related that 'it was as loud a scratching as one with long nails could make upon a Bolster'. The children lay in bed. They had become used to the noises, and were no longer so frightened by them that they could not sleep. After half an hour the scratching went into the middle of the bed to lie with the children. It was then that the sound of 'panting' was heard. The observer related that 'I put my hand upon the place, and felt the Bed bearing up against it, as if something within had thrust it up.' There were many other manifestations over the course of the next few months. One of the most remarkable was that of Mr Mompesson's horse which was found lying on the ground with one of its 'hinder Leggs in his mouth'; only with difficulty was it extracted.

In April of this year the drummer was tried at the assizes in Salisbury. He was committed to Gloucester Gaol for stealing. He was visited there one day by a Wiltshire man. The following conversation then took place.

'What news in Wiltshire?'

'I know of none.'

'No?' the drummer replied. 'Do you not hear of the Drumming at a Gentleman's house at Tedworth?'

On the release of this information the drummer was arraigned for witchcraft. At the trial the Mompesson family and many neighbours testified to the reality of the events here related. But the drummer was acquitted for lack of evidence. The manifestations eventually ceased.

The ghosts of Willington Mill

WILLINGTON IS A VILLAGE IN TYNE AND WEAR, LYING BETWEEN NORTH Shields and Wallsend. In the middle of the nineteenth century it was a busy and relatively populous neighbourhood, with a thriving flour mill – Willington Mill – owned by Messrs Unthank & Procter. Joseph Procter and his family were living in the Mill House in 1840 when a number of manifestations were heard and seen by its residents. There were thuds and scrapings, issuing from some unseen source. The sound of bare feet could be heard upon the wooden stairs. The doors of the cupboards were opened and closed for no apparent reason. There were thumps from the upper storey of the house that was never used. Mrs Procter was surprised one night when the bed in which she was lying was raised a few inches into the air.

Two of Mrs Procter's sisters were staying in the house one night, when their bed was violently shaken and the curtains around the bed were hoisted up and down. On the next night, both sisters saw a female form emerge from the wall at the head of the bed and lean over them. At other times the 'shape' of an old man or an old woman could be glimpsed; both figures were hunched over. There was also the disquieting appearance of a monkey. Another visiting relative was in the same bedroom on a later occasion. She saw what she supposed to be a white towel lying on the ground. She went over to pick it up, and was surprised to see the towel rise up from the floor, go behind the dressing table, scuttle across the room and then disappear beneath the door. This was followed by the sound of heavy footsteps descending the stairs, a noise that was heard by others in the house.

The Procters, Quakers of northern industrial stock, became accustomed to these odd phenomena. Indeed they began to take them for granted, as part of the house. But Mr Procter acquainted a friend of his with the events that had taken place. This friend, Doctor Edward Drury, decided to investigate the phenomena. He recruited a chemist from North Shields, Thomas Hudson, believing that a scientific mind was needed to explain anything untoward, and they decided to stay up all night in one of the rooms that was deemed to be 'most haunted'.

In a subsequent letter to Joseph Procter, written as a record, Doctor Drury explained what had happened. 'I took up a note which I had accidentally dropped,' he wrote, 'and began to read it; after which I took out my watch to ascertain the time. In taking my eyes from the watch they became riveted upon a closet door which I distinctly saw open, and also saw the figure of a female attired in greyish garments, with the head inclined downwards, and one hand pressed upon the chest as if in pain, and the other – the right hand – extended towards the floor with the index finger pointing downwards. It advanced with an apparently cautious step across the floor towards me. Immediately as it approached my friend, Mr Hudson, who was dozing, its right hand extended towards him. I then rushed at it, giving at the same time a most awful yell, but, instead of grasping it, I fell upon my friend. I recollected nothing distinctly for nearly three hours afterward. I have since learned that I was carried downstairs in an agony of fear and terror.'

The chemist, Mr Hudson, added to the account with the detail of 'sounds' being heard in an adjacent room. 'His horrible shouts,' he wrote, 'had made me shout in sympathy.' Doctor Drury seemed to have fainted in Mr Hudson's arms. 'I instantly laid him down and went into the room from whence the last sound was heard. But nothing was there and the window had not been opened. Mr Procter and the housekeeper came quickly to our assistance, and found the young doctor trembling in the most acute mental agony.'

The manifestations continued for some fifteen years. A clairvoyant was introduced to the house, but her only information was to the effect that the spectres 'had no brains'. They were no longer seen after the Procters left the house. Willington Mill is now part of a rope works.

Invisible blows

THE FOLLOWING ACCOUNT IS TAKEN FROM JOHN H. INGRAM'S *THE Haunted Homes and Family Traditions of Great Britain*, published in 1905.

'The village of Sampford Peverell is about five miles from Tiverton in the county of Devon; the events to be recorded occurred in 1810 and the following years, in the house of a Mr John Chave. According to the account published by the Reverend Caleb Colton, in his *Narrative of the Sampford Ghost*, some very unaccountable things had occasionally happened in this said house previous to the manifestations he makes special record of. An apprentice boy had been greatly terrified by the apparition of a woman, and he declared that he had heard some extraordinary sounds in the night; but little or no attention was paid to his statements.

'About April, 1810, however, the inhabitants of the house were alarmed by terrific noises heard in every apartment, even in the daytime. Upon anyone going upstairs and stamping on the floor in any of the rooms, say five or six times, the sounds would be repeated instantly, but louder, and generally more in number, and the vibrations of the boards caused by these repeated sounds could be sensibly felt through the soles of one's boots, whilst dust was thrown up with such velocity, and in such quantity, as to affect the eyes.

'At midday the cause of these effects would announce its approach by loud knockings in some apartment or other of the house, above or below, as the case may be. At times more than a dozen persons have witnessed these midday knockings at once. The noises would very often, and in repeated instances, follow the persons through any of the upper apartments, and faithfully answer the stamping of their feet wherever they went. If persons were in different rooms, and one stamped with his foot in one room, the sound was instantly repeated in the other. These phenomena continued day by day, almost incessantly, for about five weeks, when they gradually gave place to others still more curious and alarming.

'There were two apartments in the house in which the females who slept in them were dreadfully beaten by invisible agency. Mr Colton stated that he himself heard more than two hundred blows given in the course of a night, and he could compare them to nothing but a strong man striking with all his force, with a closed fist, on the bed. These blows left great soreness, and visible marks. Mr Colton saw a swelling, at least as big as a turkey's egg, on the cheek of Ann Mills, who voluntarily made oath that she was alone in bed when she received the blows from an invisible hand. Mrs Dennis and Mary Woodbury, also, both swore voluntarily before Mr Cotton, Mr Sully, an exciseman, and Mr Govett, a surgeon, that they were so beaten as to experience a peculiar kind of numbness, and were sore for many days after. Their shrieks while being beaten were too terrible, it is averred, to have been counterfeited.

'Mr Chave, the occupier of the house, deposed that one night the two servants were so much agitated that they refused to sleep any longer in their apartment and he therefore permitted them, in the dead of the night, to bring their bed and bed-clothes into the room where he and Mrs Chave slept. After the light had been put out, and they had been quiet about half an hour, a large iron candlestick began to move rapidly about the room. Mr Chave could hear no footsteps, but while in the act of attempting to ring the bell the candlestick was violently thrown at his head, which it narrowly missed.

'Another night Mr Searle, keeper of the county gaol, and a friend, kept watch, and they saw a sword, which they had placed near them at the foot of the bed, with a large folio Testament placed on it, thrown violently against the wall seven feet away. Mr Taylor deposed that, upon going into the room, in consequence of the shrieks of the women, he saw the sword, which had been previously lying on the floor, clearly suspended in the middle of the room with its point towards him. About a minute after it fell to the ground with a loud noise.

'Ann Mills deposed on oath that one night, while striking a light, she received a very severe blow on the back, and the tinder-box was forcible wrenched out of her hands and thrown into the centre of the room.

'The Reverend Caleb Colton said that he himself had witnessed many of the phenomena recorded above, whilst the women were in bed. Mr Colton was sure they never moved. He adds that "I have often heard the curtains of the bed violently agitated, accompanied with a loud and almost indescribable motion of the rings. These curtains, four in number, to prevent their motion, were often tied up, each in one large knot. Every curtain in that bed was agitated, and the knots thrown and whirled about with such rapidity that it would have been unpleasant to be within the sphere of their action. This lasted about two minutes, and concluded with a noise resembling the tearing of linen; Mr Taylor and Mr Chave, of Mere, being also witnesses. Upon examination, a rent was found across the grain of a strong new cotton curtain."

'Also Mr Colton heard, in the presence of other witnesses, footsteps walking by him and around him. He was, also, conscious of candles burning near him, but could see nothing. Mr Quick heard it come downstairs like a man's foot in a slipper, and seem to pass through the wall. "I have been," he says, "in the act of opening a door which was already half-open, when a violent rapping was produced on the opposite side of the same door; I paused a moment, and the rapping continued; I suddenly opened the door, with a candle in my hand, yet I swear I could see nothing. I have been in one of the rooms which has a large modern window, when, from the noises, knockings, blows on the bed, and rattling of the curtains, I really did begin to think the whole chamber was falling in. Mr Taylor was sitting in the chair the whole time; the females were so terrified that large drops stood on their foreheads. When the act of beating has appeared, from the sound of the blows, near the foot of one bed, I have rushed to the spot, but it has been instantly heard near the head of the other bed."

'Mr Colton emphasised his own statement by a voluntary affidavit, which he made in the presence of Mr B. Wood, Master-in-Chancery, Tiverton, in the course of which, he declared that, after an attendance of six nights at Mr Chave's house, during which time he had used every endeavour to discover the cause of these disturbances, and placed a seal with a crest to every door, cavity etcetera in the house through which any communication might be carried on, and having repeatedly sworn the domestics as to the truth of the phenomena, and their own ignorance of the means by which they were produced, he was still utterly unable to account for the things which he had seen and heard.

'When the manifestations ceased, if they even have now, we cannot learn; but it certainly would appear to be the case that no sure and unqualified exposure of the affair has ever yet been given.'

Old Jeffrey

Samuel Wesley, the father of John Wesley, lived with his wife and large family at Epworth Rectory in the county of Lincolnshire. He attained the post of rector in 1693, but the rectory was burned down in 1703. He rebuilt it at his own expense, although the living was a poor one.

The disturbances in the house began in 1716. The first documents of the case were written in Samuel Wesley's journal between 21 December 1716 and 1 January 1717, and a letter written by one of his daughters on 24 January. They tell the same story. The Wesley family had been 'in the greatest panic imaginable', believing that one of the Wesley sons – three of whom were away from home – had been 'by some misfortune killed'. They had received what they believed to be intimations of disaster.

At the beginning of December the maid and a man-servant, Robert Brown, 'heard at the dining-room door several dreadful groans, like a person in extremes'. There was the sound of someone knocking at the door but, on Brown opening it two or three times, there was no one there. When Brown retired to bed he heard 'as it were the gobbling of a turkey close to the bedside; and, soon after, the sound of one stumbling over his shoes and boots, but there were none there: he had left them below'.

On the next day the second maid was visited by wandering noises. She had churned some butter and, having put it on a tray, she carried it into the dairy. Whereupon 'she heard a knocking on the shelf, where several puncheons of milk stood, first above the shelf, then below'. So she 'ran away for life'.

The Wesley family laughed at them, believing the noises to be the product of their over-active imaginations. But then they also began to hear them, and Wesley's daughter reported that 'the groans, squeaks, tingling and knockings were frightful enough'. The family, with the exception of Samuel Wesley himself, also heard 'a strange knocking in divers places' but principally in the nursery. Another daughter, Emily, about twenty-two years old, was locking up the house one night, when there came a sound from the kitchen as of a large lump or lumps of coal being splintered and smashed onto the floor. She and one of her younger sisters went through the entire house, but could find nothing to explain the sound; the family pets, a cat and a dog, were sleeping peacefully in their respective places. From her bedroom Emily then heard the sound of bottles breaking beneath the stairs, when no one was in that part of the house. Another young sister, Hetty, ran in fright into her own room when she heard the sound of a man walking slowly past her in a loose and trailing gown; then 'going down the best stairs, then up the back stairs and up the garret stairs'. Soon after this the mother, Suky, heard in the corner of a room once used as a nursery 'as it were the violent rocking of a cradle, although no cradle had been there for some years'. Two of the sisters were sitting in the dining room, on a later occasion, when they heard the sound of loud raps coming from the outside of the door and on the ceiling overhead.

They eventually told their father about their experiences, of which he was unaware, but he dismissed their fears as idle. It was popularly believed that such rappings and knockings were a token of an impending death in the family, but he believed any such spectral warnings to be nonsense. Emily had meanwhile nicknamed the sprite or spirit 'Jeffrey'.

Jeffrey became more vociferous. On 21 December Mr Wesley heard him for the first time. He heard thumpings on the wall next to his bed that had no evident cause. He purchased a large mastiff, to guard against intruders, but the dog itself began to show signs of fright and unease. On the morning of 24 December Emily Wesley led her mother into a bedroom, where there were sounds of knocking on and under the bed; when Emily herself knocked on the wooden bedstead, the unknown visitant replied in kind. Then something appeared from beneath the bed. Emily said that 'it was like a badger, with no head'; Mrs Wesley simply stated that it was 'like a badger'. On the night of 25 December there was an appalling burst of noise. The dog was whining in terror as Mr and Mrs Wesley went from room to room, some locked and some unlocked; there was a thunderous noise coming from every part of the house, except for Samuel Wesley's study. On the following night Mr Wesley heard a noise that one of his daughters had also already heard. He described it as 'something like the quick winding up of a jack, at the corner of the room by my bed head'. This was followed by knocks 'hollow and loud, such as none of us could ever imitate'. The latch of the door of his study was then seen to rise and fall. When Wesley tried to enter, the door was pushed violently back against him.

'I have been with my sister Hetty,' Emily said, 'when it has knocked under her, and when she has removed has followed her.' When another sister, Kezzy, stamped her foot it imitated her.

Samuel Wesley then asked for an 'interview' with the phenomenon called Jeffrey. The rector was pushed against the door and then against the side of his desk. When he asked for an explanation he distinctly heard 'two or three feeble squeaks, a little louder than the chirping of a bird, but not like the noise of rats, which I have often heard'. A little later, when Mr and Mrs Wesley were about to enter the hall, there was a noise 'as if a very large coal was violently thrown upon the floor, and dashed all to pieces'. Samuel Wesley then called out to his wife, 'Suky, do you not hear? All the pewter is thrown about the kitchen.' When they looked there, all the pewter was in its customary place. There was then a loud knocking on the back door. Mr Wesley opened it, but saw no one. There was the same sound at the front door, but still no one stood there. After opening both doors several times, he gave up the attempt and went to bed. But 'the noises were so violent all over the house that he could not sleep till four in the morning'.

On the evening of 27 December Wesley asked a neighbouring minister, the Reverend Hoole from Haxey, to witness the strange proceedings. Hoole noted down that there were 'sounds of feet, trailing gowns, raps and a noise as of planing boards'. When Wesley travelled away on ecclesiastical business, on 30 December, the disturbances ceased. On 24 January Mrs Wesley wrote to her son that 'we are all now quiet'.

Then, on 27 March one of the Wesley daughters sent a letter to her brother Sam. 'One thing I believe you do not know,' she wrote, 'that is, last Sunday, to our father's no small amazement, his trencher [plate] danced upon the table a pretty while, without anybody's stirring the table.' She referred again to 'Jeffrey' as the agency at work. Mrs Wesley stated, in a contemporaneous letter, that it was 'beyond the power of any human being to make such strange and various noises'.

John Wesley, Samuel Wesley's more famous son, published an

entire account of the visitation some ten years later in the *Arminian Magazine*. He added the observation that the mastiff 'used to tremble and creep away before the noise began'. He also noted that certain people never heard the noises.

Vomiting coals

A PAMPHLET (NOT DATED, BUT OF THE LATE SEVENTEENTH CENTURY) — *Relation of a Wonderful Piece of Witchcraft, contained in a Letter of Master G. Clark to Mr M.T. touching a House that is Haunted nigh unto Daventree* — has the following account.

'The story is this. At Welton, within a mile of Daventry in Northamptonshire, where live together Widow Cowley, the grand-mother, Widow Stiff, the mother and her two daughters. At the next house but one live another Widow Cowley, sister to the former one, and her son, Moses Cowley, with his wife. They have a good estate in land of their own, and very civil and orderly people. These three told me that the younger of the two daughters, ten years of age, vomited in less than three days three gallons of water to their great wonder. After this the elder wench comes running, and tells them how her sister begins to vomit stones and coals. They went and were eye-witnesses, and counted them till they came to five hundred. Some weighed a quarter of a pound, and were so big, as they had enough to do to get them out of her mouth. Moses Cowley told me that he could scarce get the like into his mouth; and I do not know how any one could, if they were so big as he showed the like to me. I have sent you one, but not a quarter as big as some of them were. This vomiting lasted about a fortnight, and hath witnesses good store.

'In the meantime they threw strands of flax upon the fire, which would not blaze, though blown, but dwindled away. The bed-clothes would be thrown off the bed. Moses Cowley told me that he laid them on again several times, they all coming out of the room, and go but into the parlour again, and they were off again. And a strike of wheat, standing at the bed's feet, set it how they would, it would be thrown down again. Once the coffers and things were so transposed, as they could scarce stir about the room. Once he laid the Bible upon the bed, but the clothes were thrown off again and the Bible hid in another bed. And when they were all gone into the parlour, as they used to go together, then things would be transposed in the hall, their wheel taken in pieces, and part of it thrown under the table. In their buttery the milk would be taken off the table and set upon the ground, and once one pancheon was broken and the milk spilt. A seven-pound weight with a ring was hung upon the spigot, and the beer mingled with sand and all spoiled, and their salt mingled most perfectly with bran.

'Yet it can hardly be conceived that it was a case of imposture; or that many persons, unable to explain what they saw, would press forward to give evidence on the subject, and to maintain the accuracy of the recorded accounts, unless they had their foundation in fact.'

Broken glass

The Reverend Frederick George Lee, in his *Glimpses in the Twilight* (1884), quoted from a recent newspaper report. The name of the newspaper cannot now be ascertained.

'A series of remarkable occurrences, which have caused great excitement in the whole neighbourhood between Ellesmere, Wem, and Shrewsbury, are said to have taken place in October 1883 at a farm called "The Woods" where a farmer named Mr John Hampson resides. "The Woods" is situated about five miles from Welshampton, a mile and a half from Loppington, and nine or ten miles from Shrewsbury. With the exception of a farm about one hundred yards distant, there is no house within half a mile. It appears that as dusk was closing in on Thursday, Mrs Hampson was about to get tea ready, and put a saucepan of water on the fire for the purpose of boiling an egg. When the water began to boil Mrs Hampson placed the egg in, as usual; but the saucepan suddenly "shot", as the servants declare, off the fire into the middle of the kitchen. The cups and saucers had been arranged on the table, and one of them fell to the floor and smashed.

'Of course Mrs Hampson was a little surprised at this; but

directly afterwards when she saw the table partially turn over, apparently without being touched, and all the cups fall, she was thoroughly frightened and ran up to Mr Lea's farm. Mr Hampson had not at this time returned home from Bagley Coursing Meeting. Mr Lea at once went down, and when he arrived near the house he saw, as he describes it, "a light in all the upper windows, just as if the house was on fire". But on entering the front door and going up the stairs, all was dark. Meanwhile something had set fire to some clothes in the kitchen, and Mr Lea went in to try and put out the flames. Just then there was a noise like the report of a pistol, and the furniture and other things in the kitchen began to jump about in a manner which seemed altogether inexplicable. One of the farm-servants says, "The things began to fly about, smick, smack, the very same as if there was war!"

'Mr Lea decided to get some of the things outside, as they were being damaged, and accordingly he took hold of a barometer and carried it out. He returned, and was in the act of reaching for the gun, when he was struck by a loaf of bread, and at the request of his wife he left the house. A little cupboard in the kitchen burst open, and a bar of salt was thrown out of it onto the middle of the dairy floor. A small timepiece which stood on the mantel-shelf was thrown on the ground near the door. When Mr Hampson came home, finding it there, he placed it on a chair; and one of the servants afterwards placed it where it had stood before; and after being knocked about in this fashion, it is asserted that it was not damaged and that it did not stop.

'Mr Lea, with assistance, succeeded in getting a number of articles out of the house; and once, when he was coming out, a large kitchen table which stood under the window followed him to the door, and it probably would have gone further if the width of the door would have allowed it. On the table there stood a double-wick paraffin-lamp with a globe on it, and the globe was "lifted" off and thrown across the room, and the other part of the lamp was left standing on the table. Meanwhile things in the parlour had been taking pretty much the same course, for a volume of the *Pilgrim's Progress* came flying through the parlour door and out to the walk opposite the front door; whence, after lying there a short time, it jumped up on the window sill!

'When the mysterious affair began, a little servant-girl, aged thirteen or fourteen, whose home is at Weston, near Baschurch, was in the kitchen taking care of the child. Their clothes immediately began to singe and smoulder in patches, and the child's face and arms were burnt. The fire in the clothes of both the girl and the child was extinguished, and they set off for Mr Lea's farm; the girl taking with her two shawls which had also been burning. When she reached the farm her clothes broke out into a mass of flame, and they were torn from her body by Mrs Lea. The clothes of the child also took fire again, but it was soon put out. The two shawls began to burn again, and they were placed by someone in a small tub which was about half-full of water; but they immediately sprang out again, and were eventually kept in the tub by the weight of a pan-mug. Mrs Lea was carrying a cream-jug which Mr Hampson had won in a cavalry competition, when it suddenly leapt from her hand onto the causeway.

'Strange occurrences are said to have taken place at the neighbour's house during the evening. A plate she touched while eating her supper was apparently thrown on the floor, and the pieces were picked up by some unknown agency and placed in the centre of the table. The flower pots were carried out of Mr Hampson's house, and being placed on the grass-plot they began to move and jostle against each other. During the evening Mrs Lea went down to the house to fetch a bottle of brandy, which Mrs Hampson told her she would find in a certain cupboard; and immediately she opened the door a large dish was hurled out into the centre of the kitchen. Mrs Lea having once got the bottle at once shut the cupboard door for, as she says, "the other things were clattering".

'Other pieces of furniture were hurled into the most curious places, and a pepper-box was found the next morning on the top of the clock; while a large sewing-machine in the parlour was found very much damaged, at the opposite end of the room to that in which it formerly stood. About the time of the disturbance one of the inmates of the house was kneading some dough for baking purposes, and when things had settled a little, she was taking it to the oven, when some of the loaves were suddenly removed from the tray.

'A policeman subsequently arrived and stayed with Mr Hampson at the house all night. On Friday a large number of persons paid a visit to the house, and four policemen were there during the day, making full enquiries. Thinking there might be some kind of explosive material in the coal, they ordered it to be consumed in the open air; but it burned quietly away.

'On Saturday, just about dinner-time, the servant-girl threw some coal on the boiler fire in the dairy, when it was all thrown back again on the floor. Thomas Williams, a young farm-servant, then went to replace it, when a brick flew out from the back of the grate right across the dairy.

'The place was visited by scores of persons on Sunday.

'When our reporter visited the place yesterday it was deserted by the family, and paper-hangers were busy in the kitchen. The front windows were all broken, and there was a heap of broken pitchers and glass in the yard. Mrs Hampson and the children are staying with a relative.

'No one can explain the cause of the occurrences, and they all seem to tell a very straightforward story. The people in the neighbourhood do not appear to attribute the affair to a supernatural cause so much as might have been expected in a quiet country locality; but still they do not know how to explain it, and it is almost the only topic of conversation.'

The house in Hammersmith

ANDREW LANG WAS A FRIEND OF THE COUPLE MENTIONED BELOW, AND often visited the house in question. He tells their story in *The Book of Dreams and Ghosts* (1897), from which this summary is taken.

For fifteen years Mr and Mrs Rokeby had been living in the same old house in Hammersmith, when in the 1870s, by degrees they decided that it had become rather 'noisy'. It began with the windows being violently shaken at night, and then both of them began to hear steps where no steps should be. They were perturbed still further when they began to hear deep, long sighs at all hours of day and night. There were other odd manifestations. There were occasions when Mrs Rokeby would approach a door, when the handle would turn and the door would fly open. Andrew Lang wrote that 'I have once seen this happen, and it is a curious thing to see, when on the other side of the door there is nobody.' Then the Rokebys heard the sounds of stitching of some hard material; in her own room Mrs Rokeby heard the noise of a heavy weight being dragged across the floor, when there was no object in sight, and most alarmingly of all there were times when she experienced the sensation of her hair being pulled.

One afternoon in October 1875, at about three o'clock in the afternoon, Mrs Rokeby was sitting with three of her children in the dining room. She was reading to them. She rang the bell for the parlourmaid, when the door opened; Mrs Rokeby looked up. 'I saw the figure of a woman come in and walk up to the side of the table,' she recollected. 'She stood there a second or two, and then turned to go out again, but before reaching the door she seemed to dissolve away.' Mrs Rokeby described her as a 'grey, short-looking woman' dressed in grey muslin. 'I hardly saw the face,' she added, 'which scarcely seemed to be defined at all.' It is interesting that none of the three children saw her, and Mrs Rokeby only mentioned the event to her husband after dinner.

In the succeeding two months two servants saw the same figure in a grey dress in other rooms of the house; one saw her in the daylight, and one saw her in candlelight. Neither servant was aware of Mrs Rokeby's own experience. The two young women had become accustomed to the 'noises' within the house, but the experience of seeing the lady in grey prompted one of them to give in her notice.

Mrs Rokeby herself suffered from other manifestations. On one occasion she glimpsed a ball of brilliant light within an otherwise darkened room. She felt an icy wind in a closed room. Then the strange incidents seemed to subside, and from 1876 onwards there were only sporadic 'rappings' to remind the Rokebys of the strange events in the autumn of 1875.

Seven years later, in 1883, Mr Rokeby was away one evening. Suddenly an extraordinary volley of noises broke out throughout the entire house. Mrs Rokeby later described them as 'banging, thumping, the whole place shaking'. The dog was shut up in the library, while Mrs Rokeby took refuge in her daughter's room; the dog whined in terror as the noises increased in volume and in violence. Suddenly the noises ceased.

There was no other manifestation for several years. Then, early one evening, Mr Rokeby was smoking in the dining room with only the dog for company. Apparently for no reason the dog began to bristle up its hair, and bark at something. Mr Rokeby looked up and saw the woman in grey, with about half of her figure passed through the slightly open door. He ran to the door. There was no one there. The servants were going about their usual business, and had seen nothing.

Events at Bow

The anonymous pamphlet, *The School of Wisdom* (1783), has the following account.

'A certain gentleman, about thirty years ago, or more, being to travel from London to Essex, and to pass through Bow, at the request of a friend he called at a house there, which began then to be a little disquieted. But not anything much remarkable yet, unless about a young girl who was pluckt by the thigh by a cold hand in her bed, who died within a few days after.

'Some weeks after this, his occasions calling him back, he passed by the same house again, and had no design to give them a new visit, he having done that not long before. But it happening that the woman of the house stood at the door, he thought himself engaged to ride to her, and ask her how she did. To whom she answered, with a sorrowful countenance, that though she was in tolerable health, yet things went very ill with them, their house being extremely haunted, especially above stairs, so that they were forced to keep in the lower rooms, there was such a throwing of things up and down, of stones and bricks through the windows, and putting all in disorder.

But he could scarcely forbear laughing at her, giving so little credit to such stories himself, and thought it was only the tricks of some unhappy wags to make sports to themselves and trouble their neighbours.

'Well, said she, if you will but stay a while, you may chance to see something with your own eyes. And, indeed, he had not stayed any considerable time with her in the street, but a window of an upper room opened of itself (for they of the family took it for granted nobody was above stairs) and out comes a piece of an old wheel through it. Whereupon it presently clapt to again. A little while after, it suddenly flew open again, and out came a brick-bat, which inflamed the gentleman with a more eager desire to see what the matter was, and to discover the knavery. But none present durst accompany him. Yet the keen desire of discovering the cheat made him venture by himself into that room. Into which, when he was come, he saw the bedding, chairs, stools, and candlesticks, and bed-staves, and all the furniture, rudely scattered on the floor, but, upon search, found no mortal in the room.

'Well! he stayed there for a while to try conclusions; anon a bed-staff begins to move, and turn itself round a good while together upon its toe, and fairly to lay itself down again. The curious spectator, when he had observed it to lie still awhile, steps out to it, views whether any small string or hair were tied to it, or whether there were any hole or button to fasten any such string to; but after search he found not the least suspicion of any such thing.

'He retired to the window again, and observed a little longer what might fall out. Anon, another bed-staff rises off from the ground, of its own accord, higher into the air, and seems to make towards him. He now begins to think that there was something more than ordinary in the business, and presently [immediately] makes to the door with all speed and, for better caution, shuts it after him. Which was presently opened again, and such a clatter of chairs, and stools, and candlesticks, and bed-staves, sent after him down stairs, as if they intended to have maimed him; but their motion was so moderated that he received no harm; but by this, he was abundantly assured that it was not mere womanish fear or superstition that so affrighted the mistress of the house.

'And while in a low room he was talking with the family about these things, he saw a tobacco pipe rise from a side-table, nobody being nigh, and fly to the other side of the room, and break itself against the wall; for his further confirmation, that it was neither the tricks of the wags nor the fancy of a woman, but the mad frolics of witches and demons: which they of the house being fully persuaded of, roasted a bed-staff; upon which an old woman, a suspected witch, came to the house, and was apprehended, but escaped the law.

'But the house was afterwards so haunted in all the rooms, upper and lower, that it stood empty for a long time.'

Farewell

The excommunicate

THERE IS A CHARMING STORY CONCERNING ONE OF THE EARLIEST GHOSTS
in English literature. It comes from the late sixth century. When
St Augustine was conducting his missionary work among the Anglo-
Saxons, he came to the parish of Long Compton in Warwickshire.
The priest of the parish complained to the saint about the conduct
of the lord of the manor, who refused to pay tithes to the Church.
The priest had threatened the lord with excommunication, but the
sentence had no effect upon him. Augustine called the reprobate to
the church and summoned him to the rail where he could expostulate
with him. The lord refused to give ground on the matter. Augustine
turned away from him in order to conduct mass. Before he did so,
however, he called out in a loud voice, 'Let all those who are excom-
municate leave the church.'

So the lord left the building. As he walked into the churchyard he
saw a movement to one side of him. A grave opened up. Out of the
earth a ghost rose and began to walk away. Augustine was called to
see this strange phenomenon. He asked the ghost to stay and explain
himself. 'I was a Briton,' the ghost said. 'Saxons came and settled in
our neighbourhood. They set a Saxon priest over us. I would not pay

the tithe to the invader, and so the alien priest excommunicated me. I died soon after. On hearing your summons, however, I rose and began to walk away from the church.'

'Where is the grave of the Saxon priest?' Augustine asked him.

'Over there. It is larger than mine.'

Augustine walked over to the Saxon grave and, in the language of the saints, he raised the ghost of the dead priest. 'Absolve this man,' the saint commanded. 'Lift the taint of excommunication.'

The priest performed the simple ceremony. Ghost absolved ghost. The two spirits then returned to their rest.

The lord of the manner was so astounded, and terrified, by the scene that he became reconciled to the Church and for ever afterwards paid his tithes at the appointed time.

The killer of babies

THERE ARE MANY ACCOUNTS OF ENGLISH SPIRITS AND APPARITIONS OF the Middle Ages, the most interesting of which are to be found in Walter Map's twelfth-century anthology entitled *De Nugis Curialium*. He tells the story, for example, of a certain knight whose good and noble wife had just given birth to their first son. On the first morning after the birth the happy father went over to the cradle in which the child lay. The baby was lying in its own blood, its throat savagely cut from side to side. In the following year another child was born to them. To their extreme horror and distress, this baby was found weltering in its own blood with a gaping wound in the throat. On the third year, another newborn child was found in the same condition. It had become a house of blood.

So the wife's fourth pregnancy, in the fourth year, was heralded with charms and prayers and solemn incantations. At the time of the birth the neighbours of the knight surrounded the bed with fires and torchlight, on the common understanding that evil spirits flee fire and light. Now at the same time there arrived a pilgrim, coming to the end of his holy journey. He asked for shelter in God's name and, according to custom, was of course granted it. Whereupon he joined in the watch around the newborn child. Just after midnight, when the others had fallen asleep, he remained awake and alert.

All at once he saw the form of a tall woman stooping over the cradle; this creature reached out its hands towards the sleeping child. The pilgrim at once jumped up and seized the woman, holding her firmly until all the others had been roused. They all surrounded her with curses and execrations. She was in fact recognised by many of them as one of the richest, and noblest, women in the city. They shouted their questions at her. But she refused to answer them. She would not tell them her name. She would not tell where she lived. She stood in silence before her accusers.

The pilgrim insisted that she was an evil spirit and, taking up the key to the knight's chapel, he branded her on the face. Then he asked two of the neighbours to fetch, if they could, the lady whom they had named. Very soon after the lady was brought before them all. To their astonishment she resembled the spirit in every particular, even to the branding of the image of a key upon her face.

The pilgrim then spoke out. 'This lady who has just come in,' he said, 'is, I trust, an excellent person and dear to God: by her good works she has drawn on herself the anger of the devils, and therefore this evil emissary of theirs and minister of their wrath has been made like this good woman, and hostile to her as far as she might, in order to throw the infamy of her crime upon her. That you may see the truth of this, note what she will do when I let her go.'

He released his grip upon her arm, and at once she assumed the shape of some winged thing. It flew out of the window with appalling shrieks and cries, like the calls of a wild creature in a forest.

The young man

In 1967 Mrs D. moved to a bungalow in a small village just outside Henley; it was part of a cluster of bungalows erected in what had once been the orchard of a large mid-Victorian house. This is her story, as recorded in Anne Mitchell's *Ghosts Along the Thames* (1972).

'He appeared first in the garden one afternoon. I saw him as I looked out of the sitting-room window, a very ordinary-looking young man wearing a tweed jacket and flannels. I saw him as clearly as I am seeing you now . . . and yet I knew immediately that he was a ghost. I can't tell you how I knew; I'd never seen a ghost before, but all the same I knew he wasn't alive in the sense that you and I are alive. No, I wasn't worried by him. There was nothing ominous or threatening about his appearance. I saw him several times in the garden, and then one day I walked into my bedroom and there he was, stretched out on my sofa, under the window. This time he seemed to be in some distress, ill perhaps. I felt uneasy. I was about to speak to him when, suddenly, he disappeared. A few days later the knocking began.

'I had my ten-year-old grandchild staying with me on a long visit while her parents were abroad. She is a nervous child and she began to be disturbed by the knocking. It began gently, a rhythmic tapping, but then changed into a hard insistent knocking that was difficult to explain away. One day she complained to me that somebody had been lying on her bed. I didn't want to frighten her with questions so I don't know if she saw someone or if it was merely that the bed-clothes had been disturbed. I soothed her as best I could, but I decided that something would have to be done.'

Mrs D. called in the aid of a Unitarian minister who, on entering the house, remarked that 'Oh yes, there's someone here. But it's nothing to be frightened about. He won't harm you.' The minister spoke gently but firmly into the air, telling the young man that he was frightening the little girl and asking him to leave. The ghost never returned.

The living and the dead

The brother

THIS ACCOUNT WAS WRITTEN AT THE END OF THE LAST CENTURY BY A. Patchett Martin, the author of a memoir of Sir John Sherbroke.

'Sir John Sherbroke and General Wynyard were, as young men, officers in the same regiment, which was employed on foreign service in Nova Scotia: they were connected by similarity of tastes and studies, and spent together in literary occupation much of that vacant time which their brother officers squandered in those excesses of the table which, a century ago, were reckoned among the necessary accomplishments of the military character. They were one afternoon sitting in Wynyard's apartment; it was perfectly light, the hour was about four o'clock; they had dined, but neither of them had drunk wine, and they had retired from the mess to continue the occupations of the morning.

'I ought to have said that the apartment in which they were had two doors in it; the one opening into a passage, and the other leading into Wynyard's bedroom: there were no means of entering the sitting room but from the passage, and no other egress from the bedroom except through the sitting room; so that any person passing into the bedroom must have remained there, unless he returned by the way he entered. This point is of consequence to the story.

'As these two young officers were pursuing their studies Sherbroke, whose eye happened to glance from the volume before him towards the door that opened into the passage, observed a tall youth, of about twenty years of age, whose appearance was that of extreme emaciation, standing beside it. Struck with the appearance of a perfect stranger, he immediately turned to his friend, who was sitting near him, and directed his attention to the guest who had thus strangely broken in upon their studies. As soon as Wynyard's eyes were turned towards the mysterious visitor, his countenance became strangely agitated. "I have heard," says Sir John Sherbroke, "of a man's being as pale as death, but I never saw a living face assume the appearance of a corpse, except Wynyard's at that moment."

'As they looked silently at the form before them – for Wynyard, who seemed to apprehend the import of the appearance, and Sherbroke, perceiving the agitation of his friend, felt no inclination to address it – as they looked silently upon the figure, it proceeded slowly into the adjoining apartment and, in the act of passing them, cast its eyes with a somewhat melancholy expression on young Wynyard. The oppressing of this extraordinary presence was no sooner removed than Wynyard, seizing his friend by the arm, and drawing a deep breath, muttered in a low and almost inaudible voice, "Great God! My brother!"

'"Your brother!" repeated Sherbroke. "What can you mean, Wynyard? There must be some deception. Follow me."

'Immediately taking his friend by the arm, he preceded him into the bedroom. Imagine the astonishment of the young officers when, on finding themselves in the centre of the chamber, they perceived that the room was perfectly untenanted. Wynyard's mind had received an impression, at the moment of his first observing him, that the figure whom he had seen was the spirit of his brother. Sherbroke still persevered in strenuously believing that some delusion had been practised. They took note of the day and hour in which the event had happened; but they resolved not to mention the occurrence in the regiment, and they gradually persuaded each other that they had been imposed upon by some artifice, though they could neither account for the reasons nor suspect the author, nor conceive the means of execution; they were content to imagine anything possible, rather than admit the possibility of a supernatural appearance.

'But though they had attempted these stratagems of self-delusion, Wynyard could not help expressing his solicitude with respect to his brother, whose apparition he had seen or imagined to have seen; his frequent mention of his fears for his brother's health at length awakened the curiosity of his comrades, and eventually betrayed him into a declaration of the circumstances which he had in vain determined to conceal. The destiny of Wynyard's brother then became an object of universal and painful interest to the officers of the regiment.

'By the first ships no intelligence relating to the story could have been received, for they had all departed from England previous to the appearance of the spirit. At length the long-wished-for vessel arrived; all the officers had letters, except Wynyard. There was a solitary letter for Sherbroke still unopened; the officers had received their letters in the mess room, at the hour of supper; after Sherbroke had broken the seal of his last packet, and cast a glance on its contents, he beckoned his friend away from the company, and departed from the room.

'When he returned it was clear that his mind was filled with thoughts that manifestly pained, bewildered and oppressed him: he drew near the fireplace and, leaning his head on the mantelpiece, said in a low voice to the person nearest to him, "Wynyard's brother is no more." The first line of Sherbroke's letter was "Dear John, break to your friend Wynyard the death of his favourite brother." He had died on the day and at the very hour on which the friends had seen his spirit pass so mysteriously through the apartment.

'The reader of the above story is left in the difficult dilemma of either admitting the certainty of the facts or of doubting the veracity of those whose word it were impossible even for a moment to suspect. Sir John Sherbroke was appointed lieutenant-governor of Nova Scotia in 1811, and governor-general of British North America in 1816. General Wynyard became commander of the military forces in New Zealand and, at a later date, lieutenant-governor of New Ulster. These two gentlemen, of distinguished honour and veracity, either agreed to circulate an infamous falsehood or they were together present at the spiritual appearance of General Wynyard's brother. It is reported that "Sir John Sherbroke could not bear to hear the subject spoken of."

'This story silences the common objection that ghosts always appear at night, and are never visible to two persons at the same time.'

The summer visitor

In a letter, dated 'Highgate, March 28, 1859', Mr William Howitt sent the following narrative to Robert Dale Owen, author of *Footfalls on the Boundary of Another World*.

'The circumstance you desire to obtain from me is one which I have many times heard related by my mother. It was an event familiar to our family and the neighbourhood, and is connected with my earliest memories; having occurred about the time of my birth, at my father's house at Heanor, Derbyshire, where I was born.

'My mother's family name, Tantum, is an uncommon one. My mother had two brothers, Francis and Richard. The younger, Richard, I knew well, for he lived to an old age. The elder, Francis, was, at the time of the occurrence I am about to report, a gay young man, about twenty, unmarried, handsome, frank, affectionate, and extremely beloved by all classes throughout that part of the country.

'One fine calm afternoon my mother, shortly after a confinement, but perfectly convalescent, was lying in bed, enjoying from her window the sense of summer beauty and repose; a bright sky above, and the quiet village before her. In this state she was gladdened by hearing footsteps, which she took to be those of her brother Frank, as he was familiarly called, approaching the chamber door. The visitor knocked and entered. The foot of the bed was towards the door, and the curtains at the foot, notwithstanding the season, were drawn, to prevent any draught. Her brother parted them and looked in upon her. His gaze was earnest and destitute of its usual cheerfulness, and he spoke not a word. "My dear Frank," said my mother, "how glad I am to see you! Come round to the bedside, I wish to have some talk with you."

'He closed the curtains, as if complying; but instead of doing so, my mother, to her astonishment, heard him leave the room, close the door behind him, and begin to descend the stairs. Greatly amazed she hastily rang, and when her maid appeared she bade her call her brother back. The girl replied that she had not seen him enter the house. But my mother insisted, saying, "He was here but this instant, run! Quick! Call him back!"

'The girl hurried away, but, after a time, returned, saying that she could learn nothing of him anywhere; nor had anyone in or about the house seen him either enter or depart.

'My mother, though a very pious woman, was far from superstitious; yet the strangeness of this circumstance struck her forcibly. While she lay pondering on it, there was heard a sudden running and excited talking in the village street. My mother listened; it increased, though up to that time the village had been profoundly still; and she became convinced that something unusual had occurred. Again she rang the bell, to enquire the cause of the disturbance. This time it was the monthly nurse who answered it. "Oh it is nothing particular, ma'am," she said, "some trifling affair." Finally, however, my mother's alarm and earnest entreaties drew from her family the terrible truth that her brother had just been stabbed at the top of the village and killed on the spot.'

*

There then follows a detailed account of the event in which Francis Tantum lost his life, and Mr Howitt ends thus.

'So great was the respect entertained for my uncle, and such the deep impression of his tragic end, that so long as that generation lived the church bells of the village were regularly tolled on the anniversary of his death.

'On comparing the circumstances and the exact time at which each occurred, the fact was substantiated that the apparition presented itself to my mother almost instantly after her brother had received the fatal stroke.'

The dream of death

THIS IS THE NARRATIVE OF THE REVEREND JOSEPH WILKINS WHO, AT THE time of the events in 1754, was usher in a school at Ottery St Mary in Devon. The account was subsequently published in John Abercrombie's *Inquiries Concerning the Intellectual Powers* (1830).

'One night, soon after I was in bed, I fell asleep and dreamed that I was going to London. I thought that it would not be too much out of my way to go through Gloucestershire and call upon my family there. Accordingly I set out but remembered nothing that happened by the way till I came to my father's house; I went to the front door and tried to open it, but found it fast. Then I went to the back door, which I opened and went in; but finding all the family were in bed, I crossed the rooms only, went upstairs, and entered the chamber where my father and mother were in bed. As I went by the side of the bed on which my father lay, I found him asleep, or thought he was so; then I went to the other side, and having just turned the foot of the bed, I found my mother awake to whom I said these words: "Mother, I am going on a long journey, and am come to bid you goodbye." Upon which she answered in fright, "Oh dear son, thou are dead!"

With this I awoke, and took no notice of it more than a common dream, except that it appeared to me very perfect.

'In a few days after, as soon as a letter could reach me, I received one by post from my father; upon the receipt of which I was a little surprised, and concluded something extraordinary must have happened, as it was but a short time before I had a letter from my family, and all were well. Upon opening it I was more surprised still, for my father addressed me as though I were dead, desiring me, if alive, or whose ever hands the letter might fall into, to write immediately; but if the letter should find me living, they concluded I should not live long, and gave this as the reason of their fears.

'That on a certain night, naming it, after they were in bed, my father asleep and *my mother awake*, she heard somebody try to open the front door; but finding it fast, he went to the back door, which he opened, came in, and came directly through the rooms upstairs, and she perfectly knew it to be my step; but I came to her bedside, and spoke to her these words, "Mother, I am going on a long journey, and have come to bid you goodbye." Upon which she answered me in a fright, "Oh, dear son, thou are dead!" – which were the circumstances and words of my dream. But she heard nothing more; neither did I in my dream. Much alarmed she woke my father, and told him what had occurred; but he endeavoured to appease her, persuading her that it was only a dream. She insisted it was no dream, for that she was as perfectly awake as she ever was, and had not the least inclination to sleep since she was in bed.

'From these circumstances I am inclined to think it was at the very same instant when my dream happened, though the distance between us was about one hundred miles; but of this I cannot speak positively. This occurred while I was at the academy at Ottery, Devon, in the year 1754, and at this moment every circumstance is fresh upon my mind. I have, since, had frequent opportunities of talking over the affair with my mother, and the whole was as fresh upon her mind as it was upon mine. I have often thought that her sensations as to this matter were stronger than mine. What may appear strange is, that I cannot remember anything remarkable happening as a consequence. This is only a plain, simple narrative of a matter of fact.'

What is the matter with him?

THE NARRATOR OF THIS STORY, THE REVEREND MR MORE, WAS A FELLOW of Queen's College, Oxford, in the latter half of the eighteenth century. This is his story concerning a contemporary of the college, Mr John Bonnell, who was 'remarkable in his person and gait, and, from a peculiar manner he had of holding up his gown behind, might be recognised almost as readily by his back as by his face'. Here is Mr More's story, as published in John H. Ingram's *The Haunted Homes and Family Traditions of Great Britain* (1905).

'On Sunday, November the 18th, 1750, at noon, Mr Ballard, who was then of Magdalen College, and myself, were walking together. I was then waiting for the sound of the trumpet for dinner, and suddenly Mr Ballard cried out, "Dear me, who is that coming out of your college?" I looked and saw, as I supposed, Mr Bonnell, and replied, "He is a gentleman of our house, and his name is Bonnell; he comes from Stanton Harcourt." "Why, bless me," said Mr Ballard, "I never saw such a face in all my life." I answered slightly, "His face is much the same as it always is; I think it a little more inflamed and swelled than it is sometimes, perhaps he has buckled his band too tight, but

I should not have observed it if you had not spoken." "Well," said Mr Ballard again, "I shall never forget him as long as I live"; and appeared to be much disconcerted and frightened.

'This figure I saw without any emotion or suspicion. It came down the quadrangle, came out of the gate, and walked up the High Street. We followed it with our eyes till it came to Catherine Street, where it was lost.

'The trumpet then sounded, and Mr Ballard and I parted; and I went into the hall, and thought no more of Mr Bonnell.

'In the evening the prayers of the chapel were desired for one who was in a very sick and dangerous condition. When I came out of the chapel I enquired of one of the scholars, James Harrison, in the hearing of several others who were standing before the kitchen fire, who it was that was prayed for, and was answered, "Mr Bonnell, senior." "Bonnell senior!" said I with astonishment. "What is the matter with him? He was very well today, for I saw him go out to dinner." "You are very much mistaken," answered Harrison, "for he has not been out of his bed for some days." I then asserted more positively that I had seen him, and that a gentleman was with me who saw him too.

'This came presently to the ears of Dr Fothergill, who had been my tutor. After supper he took me aside, and questioned me about it, and said he was very sorry I had mentioned the matter so publicly, for Mr Bonnell was dangerously ill. I replied I was very sorry too, but I had done it innocently. The next day Mr Bonnell died.'

When the description of this curious episode was printed in the *Gentleman's Magazine*, after Mr More's death, Mr Ballard and the other gentlemen of Queen's College, Oxford, testified to its veracity.

The living

THERE ARE SOMETIMES INSTANCES OF SUDDEN AND SOLITARY VISIONS, which others might deem to be hallucinations. The Victorian anthologist and author Andrew Lang recounted a story told to him by an experienced and level-headed diplomat. 'This gentleman, walking alone in a certain cloister at Cambridge, met a casual acquaintance, a well-known London clergyman, and was just about shaking hands with him, when the clergyman vanished. Nothing in particular happened to either of them; the clergyman was not in the diplomat's mind at that moment.' These appearances, frequent and well attested, might be described as the ghosts of the living. There are reports of figures, seen momentarily before disappearing, that seem to emanate evil and malevolence; the seer is then confronted by the living person months or even years later.

There are also many accounts of ghosts or apparitions resuming the habitual activity in which the living person had once been engaged; an old man might be seen to cross the room and sit in a favourite armchair; a nightwatchman might resume his familiar rounds in a warehouse, his footsteps distinctly heard; a person may be seen walking on a path or street that he or she had always frequented.

And then there are the sudden apparitions, with no before and no after. On 15 December 1891, 'Mrs M' gave Andrew Lang the following account. 'One night, after retiring to my bedroom about 11 o'clock I thought I heard a peculiar moaning sound, and someone sobbing as if in great distress of mind. I listened very attentively, and still it continued; so I raised the gas in my bedroom, and then went to the window on the landing, drew the blind aside, and there on the grass was a very beautiful young girl in a kneeling posture, before a soldier in a general's uniform, sobbing and clasping her hands together, entreating for pardon. But alas he only waved her away. So much did I feel for the girl that I ran down the staircase to the door opening upon the lawn, and begged her to come in and tell me her sorrow. The figures then disappeared gradually, as in a dissolving view. Not in the least nervous did I feel then; went again to my bedroom, took a sheet of writing paper, and wrote down what I had seen.'

Such accounts are often dismissed as hallucinations or dreams so vivid that they seem altogether real to the person who has experienced them. Yet the experience of 'Mrs M' can be interpreted in a different sense. Is it possible that an event can be charged with such powerful emotion that its traces linger in the setting where it occurred? That may at least be the explanation for the ubiquitous sighting of figures beside the trees or gibbets upon which they have been hanged – unless of course popular superstition has attached presumed ghosts to these localities.

The man in the white hat

THE SURGEON-MAJOR IN ONE OF THE REGIMENTS OF THE BRITISH army, Armand Leslie, wrote the following letter to the *Daily Telegraph* in the autumn of 1881. He signed with his own name; his rank and position, so important in the nineteenth century, seem to preclude any idea of imposture or fabrication. He would not lightly have exposed himself to ridicule or censure. He would certainly not have communicated his story to the *Daily Telegraph*. He died at the battle of El Teb in the Sudan in February 1884.

'In the latter part of the autumn of 1878, between half past three and four in the morning, I was leisurely walking home from the house of a sick friend. A middle-aged woman, apparently a nurse, was slowly following, going in the same direction. We crossed Tavistock Square together, and emerged simultaneously into Tavistock Place. The streets and squares were deserted, my health excellent, nor did I suffer from anxiety or fatigue. A man suddenly appeared, striding up Tavistock Place, coming towards me, and going in a direction opposite to mine. When first seen he was standing exactly in front of my own door (5 Tavistock Place). Young and ghastly pale, he was dressed in evening clothes, evidently made by a foreign tailor. Tall and slim, he walked with long measured strides noiselessly. A tall white hat covered thickly with black crêpe, and an eyeglass, completed the costume of this strange form. The moonbeams falling on the corpse-like features revealed a face well known to me, that of a friend and relative. The sole and only person in the street beyond myself and this being was the woman already alluded to. She stopped abruptly, as if spellbound, then rushing towards the man, she gazed intently and with horror unmistakable on his face, which was now upturned to the heavens. She indulged in her strange contemplation but during very few seconds, then with extraordinary and unexpected speed for her weight and age she ran away with a terrific shriek and yell. This woman never have I seen or heard of since, and but for her presence I could have explained the incident; called it, say, subjection of the mental powers to the domination of physical reflex action, and the man's presence could have been termed a false impression on the retina.

'A week after this event, news of this very friend's death reached me. It occurred on the morning in question. From the family I learned that according to the rites of the Greek Church, and the custom of the country he resided in, he was buried in his evening clothes made abroad by a foreign tailor . . . When in England, he lived in Tavistock Place, and occupied my rooms during my absence.'

The living ghost

CHARLES HARPER, IN *HAUNTED HOUSES* (1910), RECOUNTS THE FOLLOWING.

'Three persons at East Rudham Vicarage, Norfolk, in December 1908 declared that they had seen the "ghost" of the vicar of the parish, who was at that time in Algiers.

'The vision appeared to the housekeeper, a maid-servant, and the acting vicar, the Reverend R. Brock, who gave particulars of the singular occurrence in a letter to *The Times* of December 28.

'The vicar, the Reverend D. Astley, the "living ghost", had suffered injury in a recent railway accident in Algeria, and as a consequence he was at the time in the English Hospital at Algiers.

'The housekeeper, Mrs Hartley, said that late on the Saturday afternoon she went to close the shutters in the study when she saw the vicar, Dr Astley, come across the lawn to the window.

'"He had no hat on and was smiling," she said. "He held a piece of paper in his hands. I thought he had come home unexpectedly, and opened the French windows for him to come in. He beckoned to me with the paper and then went into a little recess outside the window. I could not make out why he did not come in."

'She then called a servant and asked her if she saw anyone. "Why," said the girl, "it's Dr Astley!" She then called Mr Brock.

'The acting vicar, an elderly man, who had seen Dr Astley only once, said, "When I was called into the study, I clearly saw the figure which I recognised as that of Dr Astley. He seemed to be sitting in a chair with some books before him. I noticed his Cuddesdon collar, and his way of wearing his watch-chain straight across the waist-coat high up. The figure had the appearance of a reflection in a mirror. The time was about 4.40. With no light in the room I could see the figure quite clearly. It gradually vanished."

'A curious fact was that if Dr Astley had been sitting in his usual place in his study with a light in the room, a reflection would have appeared in the window, making him appear exactly as Mr Brock described.

'Dr Astley with Mrs Astley had left England on December 10, intending to take up the chaplaincy at Biskra for the winter months. The train in which he was travelling on December 16 from Algiers came into collision was a goods train, and the carriage in which Dr and Mrs Astley were seated was thrown over an embankment. Dr Astley was severely bruised and Mrs Astley had a leg broken and an injury to her face.'

The woman and the bird

'Sir,' Samuel Johnson said, 'it is the most extraordinary thing that
has happened in my day.' The 'thing' was the account of what became
known as 'Lord Lyttelton's ghost', although there were various accounts
of this elusive spectre. Thomas, Lord Lyttelton, was an MP who vanished
from public view after being accused of bribery; on the death of his
father he took up his title and soon became a distinctive if not neces-
sarily distinguished member of the House of Lords. He was about to
make an important speech in that assembly on Thursday 25 November
1779. The night before he had a vision, or perhaps a dream, in which
he encountered a ghost that told him he would be dead in three days.
He mentioned this to a friend, Rowan Hamilton, on the Friday of that
week – two days later. Mr Hamilton recorded the fact in his *Memoirs*.
On the same day he told another friend, Captain Ascough, and the
story was related to Mrs Thrale who immediately wrote it down in her
diary. Then Lyttelton travelled to Epsom with a party of acquaintances,
and also told them about the message of the ghost.

At about midnight on Saturday 27 November Lord Lyttelton died
suddenly in his bed, his man-servant having left his side for a moment
to bring a spoon with which to stir his medicine.

Although all the reports agree about the nature of the message delivered to him, they vary subtly in the description of the agency that brought it. It was described as a bird that turned into a woman in white, a dream of a bird followed by that of a woman, or 'a fluttering noise, as of a bird, followed by the apparition of a woman', 'a young woman and a robin' (according to Horace Walpole) or in Captain Ascough's account simply a 'spirit'.

It should be mentioned, perhaps, that Mrs Thrale made the entry in her diary before the news of Lyttelton's death reached her.

There is an intriguing postscript. On the night of 27 November a close friend of Lyttelton, an MP called Andrews, was awoken by the plain sight of Lyttelton drawing the curtains around his bed. He believed it to be a practical joke on the part of the peer but, searching the house thoroughly, he found nothing.

In the bath

Lord Brougham, who held the office of Lord Chancellor in the Whig government of Lord Grey, was a noted wit and sceptic. Nevertheless he had one experience that, as he said in his *Autobiography* (1862), 'produced such a shock that I had no inclination to talk about it'. He first noted down the details of the incident in his diary of 19 December 1799.

'At one in the morning,' he wrote, 'arriving at a decent inn [while travelling in Sweden], we decided to stop for the night, and found a couple of comfortable rooms. Tired with the cold of yesterday, I was glad to take advantage of a hot bath before I turned in. And here a most remarkable thing happened to me – so remarkable that I must tell the story from the beginning.

'After I left the High School, I went with G——, my most intimate friend, to attend the classes in the University [of Edinburgh] . . . We actually committed the folly of drawing up an agreement, written with our blood, to the effect that whichever of us died the first should appear to the other, and thus solve any doubts we had entertained of the "life after death". G—— went to India, years passed, and I had nearly forgotten his existence. I had taken, as I have said, a warm bath, and while lying in it and enjoying the comfort of the heat, I turned my head round, looking towards the chair on which I had deposited my clothes, as I was about to get out of the bath. On the chair sat G——, looking calmly at me. How I got out of the bath I know not, but on recovering my senses I found myself sprawling on the floor. The apparition, or whatever it was that had taken the likeness of G——, had disappeared . . . So strongly was I affected by it that I have written down the whole history, with the date December 19, and all the particulars as they are now fresh before me. No doubt I had fallen asleep and that the appearance presented so distinctly to my eyes was a dream I cannot for a moment doubt.'

It is in fact unlikely that Henry Brougham had fallen asleep, since he had written that he was just about to get out of the bath. On his return to Edinburgh, he received a letter from India stating that G—— had indeed died on 19 December. He remarked in his *Autobiography*, 'Singular coincidence!'

The dying mother

ON 6 JULY 1691 THE REVEREND THOMAS TILFORD, A NONCONFORMIST minister of Aylesford in Kent, sent the following letter to the Reverend Richard Baxter. Baxter included the communication in his book, *The Certainty of the World of Spirits.*

'Mary, the wife of John Goffe of Rochester, being afflicted with a long illness, removed to her father's house at West Mullin, about nine miles from her own. There she died on 4 June, this present year, 1691.

'The day before her death, she grew very impatiently desirous to see her two children, whom she had left at home to the care of a nurse. She prayed her husband to "hire a horse, for she must go home and die with the children". She was too ill to be moved, but a minister who lived in the town was with her at ten o'clock that night, to whom she expressed good hopes in the mercies of God and a willingness to die. She did express her misery, however, at being deprived of the sight of her children.

'Between one and two o'clock in the morning, she fell into a trance. One Widow Turner, who watched with her that night, says that her eyes were open and fixed and her jaw fallen. Mrs Turner put her hand upon her mouth and nostrils, but could perceive no breath. She thought her to be in a fit and doubted whether she were dead or alive. The next morning, the dying woman told her mother that she had been at home with her children.

'The nurse at Rochester, Widow Alexander by name, affirms, and says she will take her oath on it before a magistrate and receive the sacrament upon it, that a little before two o'clock that morning she saw the likeness of the said Mary Goffe come out of the next chamber (where the elder child lay in a bed by itself) the door being left open, and stood by her bedside for about a quarter of an hour; the younger child was there lying beside her. Her eyes moved, and her mouth went, but she said nothing. The nurse, moreover, says that she was perfectly awake; it was then daylight, being one of the longest days of the year. She sat up in bed and looked steadfastly on the apparition. In that time she heard the clock strike two, and a while after said, "In the name of the Father, Son and Holy Ghost, what art thou?" Thereupon the apparition removed and went away; she slipped on her clothes and followed, but what became of it she cannot tell.

'Mrs Alexander then walked out of doors till six, when she persuaded some neighbours to let her in. She told her adventure; they failed to persuade her that she had dreamed it. On that same day the neighbour's wife, Mrs Sweet, went to West Mullin, saw Mrs Goffe before her death, and heard from Mrs Goffe's mother the story of her daughter's dream of her children, Mrs Sweet not having mentioned for reasons of delicacy the nurse's story of the apparition.'

This narrative was confirmed and corroborated by Mary Goffe's father, the attending nurse and two neighbours.

Father and daughter

Here is the gist of a letter sent by the Reverend Fowler to Dr Henry Moore on 11 May 1678, and later reprinted in T. M. Jarvis's *Accredited Ghost Stories* (1823).

'This week Mr Pearson, who is a worthy good minister of this city of London, told me that his wife's grandfather, a man of great piety, and physician to the present king, his name Ferrar, nearly related and I think brother to the famous Mr Ferrar of Little Gidding – I say this gentleman and his daughter (Mrs Pearson's mother, a very pious soul) made a compact, at his entreaty, that the first of them that died, if happy, should after death appear to the survivor, if it were possible; the daughter, with some difficulty, consented thereto. Some time after, the daughter, who lived at Gillingham Lodge, fell in labour and, by mistake, being given a noxious potion, instead of the one prepared for her, suddenly died; her father lived in London and, that very night she died, she opened his curtains and looked upon him: he had before heard nothing of her illness; and, upon this apparition, confidently told the maid that his daughter was dead and, two days after, received the news. Her grandmother told Mrs Pearson this, as also an uncle of hers, and the abovesaid maid; and this Mrs Pearson I know, and this is a very prudent and good woman.'

The phantom carriage

A CORRESPONDENT CONTACTED THE REVEREND FREDERICK GEORGE LEE, the author of *Glimpses in the Twilight* (1884), to narrate the following story.

'I was staying in Brighton with some friends who were about to proceed abroad. Two ladies, a cousin and myself went out to dine at Kemp Town one evening, it being a most charming moonlight night. I told my friends I should prefer walking home to Brunswick Square (the other end of the town). I accordingly proceeded thither, on the sea side of the Esplanade.

'When just opposite the Bedford Hotel, a carriage and pair drew up alongside the rails, with two servants on the box, and an elderly lady inside. I was greatly startled as, on remarking the thing most acutely, I at once observed that the wheels made no noise.

'All at once I took about a half-dozen steps towards the carriage, to see what it meant, when I distinctly recognised the occupant as my grandmother, whom I had left perfectly well at Cheltenham a few days before; also her coachman and footman on the box.

'I at once vaulted over the rails opposite the carriage. At the same moment it struck me as most out-of-the-way that an old lady of eighty-three should bring all her belongings from Cheltenham to Brighton without informing her relatives of the move.

'As I touched the ground, I made one step forward to greet her when, to my utter astonishment and horror, the whole thing vanished.

'When I recovered myself, I went straight home and told the exact circumstances of the case.

'Of course everyone laughed at me, and sarcastically remarked that it was fortunate there were witnesses who could speak of my sobriety. I was very much put out, and hardly slept all night. Early next morning, however, we received a telegram that my grandmother had been found dead in her bed at half past seven o'clock that morning.'

The message

THE FOLLOWING ACCOUNT WAS COMMUNICATED BY SIR CHARLES LEE TO the Lord Bishop of Gloucester, soon after the events related, and was published by T. M. Jarvis in his *Accredited Ghost Stories* (1823).

'Sir Charles Lee, by his first lady, had only one daughter, of which she died in childbirth; and when she died her sister, the Lady Everard, desired to have the education of the child; and she was by her very well educated till she was marriageable; and a match was concluded for her with Sir William Perkins, but was then prevented in an extraordinary manner.

'Upon a Thursday night she, thinking that she saw a light in her chamber after she was in bed, knocked for her maid, who presently came to her; and asked her why she left a candle burning in her chamber? The maid said she left none, and there was none, but what she brought with her at that time. Then she said it was the fire: but that the maid told her it was quite put out, and said she believed it was only a dream; whereupon she said it might be so, and composed herself again to sleep.

'About two of the clock she was awaked again, and saw the

apparition of a little woman between her curtain and her pillow, who told her she was her mother, and that she was happy, and that by twelve of the clock that day she should be with her; whereupon she knocked again for her maid, called for her clothes, and when she was dressed went into her closet, and came not out again till nine; and then brought out a letter sealed to her father, brought it to her aunt, the Lady Everard, told her what had happened, and desired that as soon as she was dead it might be sent to him.

'The lady thought she was suddenly fallen mad, and thereupon sent presently away to Chelmsford for a physician and surgeon, who both came immediately. The physician could discern no indication of what the lady imagined, or of any indisposition of her body; notwithstanding the lady would needs have her let blood, which was done accordingly; and when the young woman had patiently let them do what they would with her, she desired that the chaplain might be called to read prayers, and when prayers were ended, she took her guitar and psalm-book, and sat down in a chair without arms, and played and sang so melodiously that her music-master, who was then there, admired at it. Near the stroke of twelve, she rose and sat herself down in a great chair with arms, and presently fetching a strong breathing or two, immediately expired, and was so suddenly cold as was much wondered at by the physician and surgeon. She died at Waltham in Essex, three miles from Chelmsford; and the letter was sent to Sir Charles, at his house in Warwickshire: but he was so afflicted with the death of his daughter that he came not till she was buried; but when he came he caused her to be taken up, and to be buried by her mother at Edmundton, as she desired in her letter. This was about the year 1662 or 1663.'

The uncle

An anonymous pamphlet of 1783, *The School of Wisdom*, has the following story.

'Mr Joseph Glew, a sword-hilt-maker, lived with his wife (both ancient people) for many years, and one woman lodger, in the house over the archway in the passage to Bear-yard, near the Oratory, in Lincoln's-Inn-fields; and for the sake of the company desired a nephew of his, by marriage, to come and lodge in his house. Accordingly in the beginning of January, 1739–40, the nephew came to his uncle and spent every evening with him and his wife in reading etcetera for their amusement.

'About the twenty-fifth of the same month, after the nephew had been reading to his uncle and his aunt, who were at this time in very good health, some meditations out of Dr Thomas Coney's *Devout Soul*, he retired to his chamber, a large back room, up two pair of stairs, and having fastened the door, went to bed and fell asleep before ten o'clock. A little before the clock struck twelve, he was awakened by the drawing of the curtain of his bed, and, starting up, saw by a glimmering light, resembling that of the moon, the shadow of his uncle in the nightgown and cap he had on when he last parted with him, standing on the right side, near the head of the bed, holding the head curtain back with his left hand, and seemed as if he was about to strike or stroke him with his right; but the nephew believed the latter, as the face had a cheerful look, and they lived in the greatest amity.

'At this instant Mrs Cooke, an ancient woman, that lodged in the fore two pair of stairs rooms, and who formerly belonged to Mr Rich's company of comedians several years, came out of her apartment to light down stairs the widow of the facetious James Spiller, who had been this evening to visit her. The nephew now heard the clock, which was in his uncle's apartment underneath, strike twelve, and tried to call out to the two women as they passed by his door, but he had lost all power of utterance. The ghost kept its position, and the nephew his eyes fixed on it, and heard, when the two women opened the street door, that they called to the watchman, as he came by crying the hour of twelve, and agreed to give him some pence to light Mrs Spiller to her lodging, which was but at a little distance. On which she went away, and Mrs Cooke, having again fastened the door, was coming up the stairs, when the nephew supposed he swooned away; for, on coming again to his use of reason, he found himself half out of bed, and immersed in a cold and sickly sweat. The first thing he heard, after he had recovered from his fright, was the clock striking one. He now wrapped himself in his bed-clothes, but closed his eyes no more the whole night.

'About eight in the morning, as soon as he heard his aunt open the door of her apartment, he jumped out of bed and, putting on his apparel with what expedition he could, hurried down to her room, and, having asked how she did, heard she was pretty well. On this he told his aunt what he had seen, with the time, and the circumstances; but she, looking on it as fabulous, they called for Mrs Cooke, who was just got up, and she confirmed everything he had said concerning Mrs Spiller and the watchman, a positive proof he was awake and in his senses.

'The aunt now desired that he would not mention it to his uncle, which he promised he would not, but withal he told her that he could never more lie in that chamber, and went out about his business. The same day, before one o'clock, the nephew received a message from his aunt, where he was at work in Fleet-street, desiring him to come immediately to her: he accordingly went to her house, where he found his uncle dead, and was told that he fell down in crossing his room, and died suddenly about three minutes before twelve o'clock; exactly twelve hours from his ghost's appearance to his nephew.

'The circumstances induced the young man to think his uncle might want to reveal something to him, and therefore desired to sit up with his corpse the night preceding his interment, which the aunt agreeing to, he fortified his mind, and prepared a devotional book for his companion, with which he shut himself up in the room with the body, about six in the evening, in hopes he might see the spirit of his uncle, if he had anything to say or to open to him; but as nothing occurred, during fourteen hours he was alone with the corpse, the following evening he attended his funeral to the north part of the church-yard of Saint Giles's in the Fields.'

The story of John Donne

IZAAK WALTON WROTE THE FOLLOWING IN HIS LIFE OF JOHN DONNE.

'In the year 1612, Dr Donne accompanied Sir Robert Drury to Paris; where he is said to have had a most extraordinary vision: When Sir Robert requested him to go, Mrs Donne, who was then with child, expressed an unwillingness, saying "that her divining soul boded some ill in his absence". But, upon Sir Robert's being importunate, she at last consented.

'Two days after their arrival, Dr Donne was left alone in a room, in which Sir Robert, and he, and some other friends, had dined together: to which Sir Robert returning in an hour, as he left, so he found Dr Donne alone, but in such an ecstasy, and so altered in his countenance, that Sir Robert could not look upon him without amazement. He asked him, in God's name, what had befallen him in the short time of his absence. Dr Donne was not able to answer directly, but, after a long and perplexed pause, did at last say, "I have seen a dreadful vision since I saw you: I have seen my dear wife pass twice by me through this room, with her hair hanging about her shoulders, and a dead child in her arms. This I have seen since I saw you."

'To which Sir Robert answered, "Sure, sir, you have slept since I went out, and this is the result of some melancholy dream, which I desire you forget, for you are now awake." Dr Donne answered, "I cannot be surer that I now live, than that I have not slept since I saw you; and am as sure, that at her second appearing, she stopped, looked me in the face, and vanished."

'A servant was immediately dispatched to Drury-house, to know whether Mrs Donne was still living and, if alive, in what condition; who brought word that he found and left her very sad and sick in her bed and that, after a long and dangerous labour, she had been delivered of a dead child. And, upon examination, the abortion proved to be on the same day, and about the same hour, that Dr Donne affirmed he saw her pass by him in the room.'

Bibliography

Abercrombie, John, *Inquiries Concerning the Intellectual Powers* (1830)

All the Year Round, 24 December 1870

Anon., *The School of Wisdom* (1783)

Armitage, Harold, *The Haunted and the Haunters* (1925)

The Athenaeum, January 1880

Baring-Gould, Sabine, *Yorkshire Oddities* (1974)

Baxter, Richard, *The Certainty of the World of Spirits* (1691)

Bede, the Venerable, *Ecclesiastical History of the English People* (731)

Bovet, Richard, *Pandaemonium, or the Devil's Cloyster* (1684)

Briggs, Katharine M., *The Folklore of the Cotswolds* (1974)

Brockie, William, *The Legends and Superstitions of Durham* (1886)

Collins, B. Abdy, *The Cheltenham Ghost* (1948)

Crowe, Catherine, *The Night Side of Nature* (1848)

Daily Mail, 21 December 2007

Deane, Tony, *The Folklore of Cornwall* (1975)

Bibliography

Dingwall, E. J. and Hall, T. H., *Four Modern Ghosts* (1958)

Dutton, Ralph, *A Hampshire Manor* (1968)

Evening Standard, 23 December 1953

The Gentleman's Magazine (1774)

Goss, Michael, *The Evidence for Phantom Hitch-Hikers* (1984)

Harper, Charles, *Haunted Houses* (1910)

Howitt, William, *History of the Supernatural* (1863)

Hull Advertiser, 13 August 1818

Ingram, John H., *The Haunted Homes and Family Traditions of Great Britain* (1905)

Jarvis, T.M., *Accredited Ghost Stories* (1823)

Lang, Andrew, *The Book of Dreams and Ghosts* (1897)

Lang, Andrew, *The Making of Religion* (1898)

Lee, Revd Frederick George, *Glimpses in the Twilight* (1884)

Lindley, Charles, Viscount Halifax, *Lord Halifax's Ghost Book* (1936)

McEwan, Graham J., *Haunted Churches of England* (1989)

Map, Walter, *De Nugis Curialium*, ed. M. R. James (1914)

Martin, A. Patchett, *Memoir of Sir John Sherbroke* (1893)

Mitchell, Anne, *Ghosts Along the Thames* (1972)

Moss, Peter, *Ghosts over Britain* (1977)

Mullen, Peter, *Holy and Unholy Ghosts* (1995)

Newton, John (ed.), *Early Modern Ghosts* (2003)

Nicholson, John, *Folk Lore of East Yorkshire* (1890)

Noakes, Ben, *I Saw a Ghost* (1986)

Notes and Queries, 1880, 1904

O'Donnell, Elliott, *Haunted Houses of London* (1909)

Owen, Robert Dale, *Footfalls on the Boundary of Another World* (1860)

Palmer, Kingsley, *Oral Folk Tales of Wessex* (1973)

Palmer, Roy, *The Folklore of Warwickshire* (1976)

Playfair, Guy Lion, *This House is Haunted* (1981)

Price, Harry, *The Most Haunted House in England* (1940)

Price, Harry, *The End of Borley Rectory* (1946)

Proceedings of the Society for Psychical Research, vol. xii (1883)

Relation of a Wonderful Piece of Witchcraft contained in a letter of Master G. Clark to Mr M. T. touching a House that is Haunted nigh unto Daventree (n.d. [late 17th century])

Retford, Worksop and Gainsborough News, 10 March 1883

Richardson, M. A., *The Local Historian's Table Book* (1846)

Sinclair, George, *Satan's Invisible World Discovered* (1685)

Spicer, Henry, *Strange Things Among Us* (1863)

State Papers, Domestic: Charles I, vol. 383, no. 5

Tegner, Henry, *Ghosts of the North Country* (1974)

Townsend, the Marchioness, and Ffoulkes, Maude, *True Ghost Stories* (1936)

Walton, Izaak, *Lives of John Donne, Henry Wotton etc.* (1825)

Wiltshire, Kathleen, *Ghosts and Legends of the Wiltshire Countryside* (1973)